Welcome to the
Episcopal Church

Welcome to the Episcopal Church

*An Introduction
to Its History,
Faith, and Worship*

Christopher L. Webber

Foreword by
The Most Reverend Frank T. Griswold III
Presiding Bishop and Primate

MOREHOUSE PUBLISHING

Morehouse Publishing
P.O. Box 1321
Harrisburg, PA 17105

Morehouse Publishing is an imprint of Church Publishing Incorporated.

Printed in the United States of America
Cover design by Corey Kent

Library of Congress Cataloging-in-Publication Data

Webber, Christopher.
    Welcome to the Episcopal Church : an introduction to its history, faith, and worship / Christopher L. Webber ; forward by Frank T. Griswold III.
        p. cm.
    Includes bibliographical references.
    ISBN 0-8192-1820-0 (pbk. : alk. paper)
    1. Episcopal Church. I. Title.
BX5930.2 . W43 1999
283'.73—dc21   99-045138

Contents

Foreword

Most Episcopal churches have a sign saying, "The Episcopal Church Welcomes You," and certainly the clergy and laity of parishes do their best to welcome those who come to services for the first time. Episcopalians, on the whole, are very friendly people. We love to show hospitality to those who come for a visit, and we hope they will return. We do this also because we believe that hospitality to a guest is one small sign that we can make of the much more generous hospitality that God shows to those seeking to know the risen Christ.

Christopher Webber has written a helpful introduction to the history, faith, and worship of the Episcopal Church which will be one more way we can make newcomers welcome to our church. It will also be useful to those already active in our church community.

The author writes from the perspective of scholar, teacher, overseas worker and pastor of a variety of churches as he tells the story of the Episcopal Church: who we are, where we have come from, what we believe, and how we worship God. What especially pleases me is that the book makes clear that the worship of God is the most important thing that can be said about us, and that worship is the source for everything else in our life together—our commitment to justice for all people, our mission to those who do not yet know Jesus Christ as their Lord and Savior, and how we should live out our lives in this very complex world.

Being a Christian, in fact being a religious person at all, is not easy in our present society. All of us are pulled in many directions. This book makes it clear that the Episcopal Church does not offer any final or absolute answers to the conflicts in ourselves or in our society. It does, however, affirm that as a community grounded in prayer and worship, we are seeking to know God's will and, by the grace of God, to do God's will in all the areas of human concern that are the responsibility of those of us who believe in Jesus Christ.

It is obvious that this book has come from one who, over the years of his pastoral leadership, has seen the need for study and growth to achieve a fullness in Christ. I hope that you who read it will gain a better understanding of the Episcopal Church and a fuller knowledge of our faith community.

The Most Reverend Frank T. Griswold III
Presiding Bishop and Primate

Preface

There is probably no church sign more often seen and widely recognized on American streets and highways than the one that says, "The Episcopal Church Welcomes You." Perhaps it was even one of these signs that brought you to the Episcopal Church. But whether you have been sitting in the pews for many years or are new in the last few weeks or months, the sign is true: The Episcopal Church welcomes you.

Being welcoming, of course, is not just a matter of a warm greeting from an usher or a friendly reception at the coffee hour. Part of the process of hospitality is learning each other's stories. As you meet people in the coffee or Christian Education hours, or in committee meetings or church activities, you will probably begin to tell people a little about who you are, how you came here, and what you believe. You may even begin to explore and share your own deeply held beliefs about prayer, the Bible, and God. Engaging in these conversations will help make the Church into "home" for you. These same conversations will also be an important part of your growth and participation in this community.

Another part of your journey in the Church is learning its stories: where it came from, what it believes, how it worships, how it understands the Bible and God, how it reaches out to the rest of the world. Many of these stories are contained in this book. Some of them may have much in common with your own story, and may help you understand why you were drawn here, and how your story might become a part of the larger story. One thing you will notice right away, however, is that our history, beliefs, and even our governing structure take a variety of perspectives and voices into account. The words "inclusive" and "diverse" appear often in the mission statements of individual Episcopal parishes, as well as in the materials from our national offices. Episcopalians value what is revealed about God and God's will in the continuing conversation among people of a variety of perspectives. It is why our signs say: "The Episcopal Church welcomes you." I hope you enjoy the conversation!

It would be hard for any single individual to capture the diversity of the Episcopal Church in writing. No single individual could experience in a lifetime the varieties of ways in which the Anglican vision is lived out in thousands of parishes spread across the country and around the world. I have been greatly helped, however, by the careful reading and suggestions of a number of individuals, among them Debra Farrington, Donald Hamer, Margaret Webber, Brother Randolph Horton, and the Revs. G. Scott Cady, Hope Eakins, William Gregg, and Daniel Hardy. They have helped me describe the Episcopal way of life more accurately, though not always, I must admit, as they might have described it themselves. The final balance, accurate or not, remains my own. But this book is intended only as in introduction and starting point. Finally, each individual will need to make a personal investigation and arrive at his or her own understanding. There is much more—always—for each of us to find.

History

BEGINNINGS

When a baby is born, the grandparents and cousins and friends will come to admire the new member of the family and someone will say, "Isn't she the very image of Great-aunt Abigail!" or, "Doesn't he look just like Uncle Fred?" For better or worse, we inherit many of our characteristics from our ancestors. Churches, like people, are shaped by their past.

But how far back must we go to understand the Episcopal Church? As members of an American church, we need to know what happened in the colonial period and Revolution, but as inheritors of a European tradition, we can't avoid dealing with the church's English heritage also. Finally we will need to go still further back and understand something about the Reformation and the Middle Ages and the early church. If we had time, perhaps we should talk about Adam and Abraham! But this book is an introduction to the American Episcopal Church, so we will need to concentrate on the last few centuries of our history and take time here for only a few comments about the early church, Middle Ages, and Reformation. What we need to look for in a quick summary of our church ancestry is the common characteristics that have always been part of the church's life and still are today. Let's begin with the Bible.

The Bible tells us that the first Christians "devoted themselves to the apostles' teaching and fellowship, to the breaking of bread and the prayers" (Acts 2:42). If that is a thumbnail description of the early church, then, in a church descended from the apostles, we should expect to find that the breaking of bread and prayer are still at the center of the church's life, that a relationship with the apostles is still evident, and that our faith today is still rooted in their teaching.

Episcopalians claim that the very name of the church indicates our continuation of apostolic tradition. The apostles were overseers of the church, and the name "Episcopal" (from the Greek *episcopos* or overseer) indicates that we are a church that believes bishops, as successors to the apostles, are a vital aspect of our common life. The Prayer Book (p. 510) tells us that the church has had "three distinct orders of ordained ministers," bishops, priests, and deacons, since the time of the apostles. That the Episcopal Church maintains this tradition links us strongly with the church in all ages. It also provides a common bond with the Roman Catholic and Orthodox Churches of today.

Why is it, then, that there are so many churches around us that do not share this pattern? What is it that separates us from our fellow Christians in other Christian churches, both those with bishops and those without? To understand these divisions, we need to look briefly at the Middle Ages and especially at the Reformation of the church that took place in the sixteenth century.

THE REFORMATION

The church that grew up in the Roman Empire survived the empire's collapse and became the primary civilizing force in western Europe for almost a thousand years. The monasteries, cathedrals, and parish churches were centers of light and learning, teaching faithfulness and compassion in a chaotic and generally savage world. But to hold on to the faith in such a world and avoid destruction, the church had to resist change and to exalt its own authority in every aspect of life—a policy that became increasingly difficult to maintain. As the nation-states of modern Europe began to emerge, increasing conflict between the old order and the new led to an explosion, which we know as the Reformation. Many of the factors that contributed to that divisive explosion were the very ones that had united the church of the Middle Ages, matters of church government, language, and culture. Others were deeper matters of faith that might have been dealt with peacefully if political and economic considerations had not complicated the picture.

At the heart of the matter were concerns for unity and power. The church had maintained its unity in the Middle Ages by the use of Latin as a common language, but the people of Europe in the sixteenth century spoke French, English, Spanish, German, and other languages as well. The church had maintained its unity by training the clergy as an educated elite, but growing commercial opportunities required an educated laity. The church had maintained its unity by educating clergy to teach the faith, but the invention of the printing press and a better-educated laity made it possible for others to read the Scriptures and to raise questions about the differences they saw between the church of the apostles and the church around them. The church had maintained its unity by appointing bishops who were, in effect, the local agents of the Bishop of Rome; through them money flowed to Rome to enable it to maintain the structure that had been so crucial to the survival of western civilization, but now there were national rulers who wanted that money for their own purposes. The Reformation was not

only about changes in the church, it was also about a new economic order, the role of educated lay people, and the authority of secular rulers in conflict with the authority of the pope.

In the turmoil of reformation, the role of bishops as
guardians of the faith was hard to distinguish from their role as
representatives of papal government. In northern Europe,
where independence from papal government was as much an
issue as was a reformed faith, the bishops were seen as
nonessential aspects of the church's life and even as obstacles to
the creation of a renewed and purified church. In England,
however, geo-graphy and personalities shaped a different out-
come. As an island in a distant corner of Europe, England was
somewhat insulated from the full force of the Reformation. As
a unified territory under the strong rule of Henry VIII, the
English church was held back from following the teachings of
Luther and Calvin, the leaders of the Reformation on the continent. Had it not been for a personal quarrel between Henry
and the pope, the English church might have remained under
Roman rule; indeed, Henry had written a criticism of Luther's
teaching that so pleased the pope that he had conferred on
Henry the title "Defender of the Faith." The separation
between Rome and England took place afterwards for political
reasons, not theological, and was designed to give Henry,
rather than the pope, final authority in England. The reformation that took place in England afterwards was far more
moderate and gradual than that on the continent. The Church
of England, once separated from papal government, became a
reformed church, but it was not as radically changed in its
structures, practices, and teaching as the reformed churches of
continental Europe. Bishops still served as overseers of the
church, but now they served by appointment of the crown
rather than the pope. The Church of England also became a
church that worshiped in English, the language of the people,

and in which people were permitted to receive the wine as well as the bread in Holy Communion. The same bishops and priests still ministered the same sacraments in the same cathedrals and parish churches, but the vital importance of the individual's faith and the intelligent participation of the people in worship as in the early days of the church were affirmed. Most important of all, the English church, like the reformed churches of Europe, made it clear that salvation comes through God's grace and the faith of the believer, not through human merit or achievement. The church in England was also defined more by a common Prayer Book and pattern of worship than by a pope or a statement of doctrine. This reformed catholic church was then carried out from England by colonists and missionaries to the New World, which was just beginning to be explored and colonized.

THE CHURCH IN THE COLONIES

The first tentative English contact with the New World began with a round-the-world cruise by Sir Francis Drake. Putting ashore in San Francisco Bay in 1579, Drake's chaplain conducted the first Prayer Book service in the present territory of the United States on its western coast. The spot is marked today by what is known as "the Prayer Book Cross." But, of course, it was on the east coast that the first European efforts were made to settle the newly discovered land. An ill-fated colony planted at North Carolina, Virginia, disappeared mysteriously, but before it disappeared, Virginia Dare became the first child baptized in this country. The service was conducted on August 18, 1587, out of the Book of Common Prayer.

The first permanent settlement was made at Jamestown in 1607, and the colonists brought a chaplain named Robert Hunt to lead them in worship. With a sail for an awning and a plank nailed between two trees for a pulpit, they made themselves a church and planted the seed from which the Episcopal Church grew. But Anglicanism in the New World would become something very different from what it had been in England. Here the governor and House of Burgesses filled some of the roles played by the crown, the bishops, and the parliament in England, but the church had to develop new ways of life since the governor could not exactly be a bishop. What happened in Virginia was that each community organized itself as a parish with a vestry to administer it, voted taxes to pay for a church, and then imported a priest from England. As a result, without any plan for it to do so, church life in Virginia developed a democratic, congregational style of government. Church members called themselves Anglicans, but the nearest bishop was in England—and the colonists rather liked it that way. It was, of course, a nuisance to send young men to England to be ordained or to import older men already ordained, but bishops were still thought of as an arm of the government, and the colonists didn't mind keeping the various arms of English government at a distance. They were learning that democracy was enjoyable.

Meanwhile, to the north, New England began to be settled by dissenters from the Church of England. There had always been some who were not satisfied with a moderate reformation and who yearned for the more radical reforms of Calvin's followers. Failing to attain their goals in England, they migrated to the New World and, with a charter from the king that made them still part of England, they established a church-state in Massachusetts without either Prayer Books or bishops to impede them. Yet New England was royal territory and not all those who came were inspired by Calvinist teaching. Many merchants and traders and farmers came simply to find new opportunity, and the Church of England felt it important to provide clergy for them. Societies were formed to raise funds

and support the missionaries who came out, and slowly the
Church of England established a minority presence in the
northern colonies.

The Anglican Church in New England, however, had a very
different style from that in Virginia. In New England, the support of the government went to the Congregational Church,
not the Church of England. Support for Anglican clergy, therefore, came from the societies in England, and the Anglicans in
New England, quite unlike those in the south, valued their ties
with England and their distinctive identity as Anglicans in a
Calvinist society. In an odd reversal, the Anglicans in Virginia,
though established by act of the House of Burgesses, developed
a congregational style of life, while the Puritans, who had fled
the established church in England, created an established,
though congregational, church in the New World.

THE REVOLUTION

The American Revolution tested the identity of these New
World Anglicans and created something new out of the fire of
conflict. For members of the church in the southern colonies,
the new situation created the possibility of a different type of
church entirely separated from the state and freed of all the old
traditions that seemed out of place in an enlightened age.
Thomas Jefferson even rewrote the Bible, leaving out passages
that he thought were no longer relevant or credible. Many of
these southern leaders imagined an American church controlled entirely by the laity, without bishops or prayer books or
complicated creeds, with clergy who would exhort people to
behave themselves and to maintain a proper, if distant, relationship with their Benevolent Creator. Under their influence,
the first proposed American Prayer Book left out the Nicene
Creed, shortened the Apostles' Creed, and dropped references
to being born again from the baptismal liturgy.

New England Anglicans had a different view of things. Many of them had fled to Canada at the onset of revolution; others found their churches closed by mobs and themselves tarred and feathered for daring to continue using their prayer books with the prayers for the king and royal family. When the war was over, those who remained saw that they would have to take radical steps if their pattern of life and worship was to survive in any recognizable form. First of all, they believed, they needed bishops. The clergy of Connecticut met and chose one of their number, Samuel Seabury, to go to England to seek consecration as a bishop. What Seabury found on arriving in London in 1784 was that the English bishops could not take that step. In the first place, the existing laws of England required an oath of loyalty to the king, which Seabury obviously could not take. And, in the second place, the English bishops were very doubtful that it was right to send a bishop out to a territory where the government would not impose taxes to support him. They could not imagine that people would support bishops of their own free will.

Seabury did, however, have an alternative. Although England had followed its own path at the Reformation, the majority of the Scottish people had become followers of Calvin and established a Presbyterian Church. But some in Scotland had resisted the Calvinist majority and created a small, unestablished church with its own Prayer Book and bishops. They knew that it was possible to maintain an Anglican identity with bishops and without taxes, and they were willing to consecrate Samuel Seabury. The Scottish bishops did, nonetheless, exact certain promises of Seabury. He must, they insisted, do all in his power to shape the American Prayer Book to be like theirs. And, in particular, they commended to him an invocation of the Holy Spirit in the Eucharistic prayer. They had borrowed the practice from the

Eastern Orthodox liturgy and believed it was truer to the
ancient pattern of Christian worship. The Prayer Book of the
new American church would have links not only to Scotland
but also to the Eastern Orthodox Church.

When Seabury returned, the next question to face was
whether the former members and clergy of the Church of
England in the colonies could be united to form one new
national church. It wasn't easy. Virginia was accustomed to
doing without bishops altogether and being governed by the
laity, while the New Englanders had been governed by the clergy and the missionary societies in England without much
involvement of laity. The first proposal for a General
Convention of the church included no separate house of bishops. Connecticut church leaders said they would not join under
those conditions. For a while it seemed as if New England
Anglicans would not come into a church that gave laity any significant role and Virginia Anglicans would not come in if bishops were to govern. Fortunately there were representatives of the
"Middle Colonies," New York, Delaware, Maryland, and
Pennsylvania, led by William White of Pennsylvania, who provided a moderating influence and worked out, in sometimes
heated negotiations, a constitution that provided a separate
house of bishops with the right to review and veto but not to
initiate, and a lower house in which all the dioceses would be
represented by equal numbers of clergy and laity.

Then the problem facing the church was what bishops
would do between conventions. Americans had had a church
without bishops for almost two centuries. Now that they had
bishops, they would have to work out what they were for. At
first, the new bishops served as rectors of larger parishes and
visited the other parishes occasionally to confirm candidates.
Gradually various administrative duties were added and bishops
were freed from parish responsibilities. Over time, Episcopal

bishops have won a place for themselves as leaders and chief pastors, but their administrative powers are still carefully balanced by elected clergy and lay representatives. Episcopal bishops may wear vestments that make them look authoritative, but they function in a much more collegial manner than do bishops in other traditions. And that is a result of the church's colonial heritage.

A New Beginning

Having built the structure, it remained to be seen whether anyone would come. Some were quite certain they would not. Sadly diminished in numbers, cut off from English assistance and prohibited from using taxes any more for their support, it seemed to some that this remnant of the Church of England would fade away in a generation. That it did not was due to a new generation of leaders who were convinced, in spite of appearances, that the church could not only survive but grow.

They were right. By 1835, the Episcopal Church was ready not only to maintain itself but to launch out in mission. The General Convention of that year proclaimed that the entire church was a missionary society and sent out missionaries to the new territories in the Midwest (another first—bishops for areas where there were still no churches) and even, following St. Paul's example, to Greece.

Four men might be selected to illustrate the spirit of this new and lively American church: John Henry Hobart, Jackson Kemper, Absalom Jones, and William Augustus Muhlenberg.

Hobart, elected as Bishop of New York in 1816, was a man of enormous energy and enthusiasm. If you read the story of his life and ministry, you find yourself worn out by his activity and not surprised to find that he died at the age of 56. He was a prolific writer and constant organizer. In 1817, he founded the General Theological Seminary, the oldest seminary in the

Anglican Communion, as a school to teach his views to a new generation of clergy. He also founded a Prayer Book society and a mission society, and he traveled constantly to build up the church. On one visitation in western New York State, he covered fifteen hundred miles in thirty days over roads so bad he frequently had to get out of his carriage and walk. But he believed in episcopacy and did what he could to propagate it. He wrote, "Without [episcopacy] there can be no visible ministry, no visible sacraments, no visible church." His motto, "evangelical faith and apostolic order," summed up all that was best and most hopeful in the resurgent life of the church in the first part of the nineteenth century.

Those same years also saw the new nation expanding westward, and the church rallied itself to send out missionary bishops. The General Convention of 1835 appointed Jackson Kemper (1789–1870) as Bishop of Indiana and Missouri and shortly added Wisconsin and Iowa. Despite this enormous jurisdiction, he was able to carry out his mission effectively, establishing churches in areas where settlement was only beginning and the Episcopal Church was unknown. Kemper had a vision of the church raising up a native ministry on the frontier. Three men, just completing their studies at General Seminary, responded to his vision and founded Nashotah House, a new seminary in Wisconsin, giving its life a monastic pattern long before monastic life was reestablished in the Anglican Communion. The students rose at 5 A.M., recited the monastic hours, had weekly Communion, supported themselves by physical labor, and evangelized the countryside for miles around. Before Kemper's death thirty-five years later, he had organized six dioceses, consecrated a hundred churches, and ordained two hundred men to carry out the ministry of the church in the west.

Additional evidence of the church's innate strength and appeal lies in the work of Absalom Jones (1746–1818), the

first African-American priest of the Episcopal Church. He and
a friend named Richard Allen had served as evangelists and
built up the Black membership of St. George's Methodist
Church in Philadelphia, but one day they were directed by the
ushers to sit in the gallery. They refused to go and decided to
found churches where they would not be second-class citizens.
Allen founded the African Methodist Church but Jones joined
the Episcopal Church, founded St. Thomas' Church, and was
ordained a deacon and then, in 1802, a priest. More than sixty
years before the Emancipation Proclamation, Jones was able to
exercise a leadership role in the church and to found a parish
that is still a center of mission and service. Equally striking was
Jones's heroism during the great yellow fever epidemic of 1794
in Philadelphia. It was one of the worst epidemics ever to hit
an American city and no one knew what to do. Blood letting
was still the common cure for fever and, of course, it weakened
the victims further. Hundreds were dying and there was no
one even to carry away the bodies until Jones came forward
and volunteered to find people to do it. During the worst of
the epidemic it was Jones and his companions who saw to it
that the dead were buried and that life in the city of
Philadelphia did not disintegrate completely.

Another example of the growing strength of the church was
the work of William Augustus Muhlenberg (1796–1877),
who sparked off more new kinds of ministry in his one life
than might have been expected from the whole church. He
had served at St. George's, Flushing, Long Island, and had
begun there a boys' academy that inspired, among others, the
founding of St. Paul's, Concord, New Hampshire, and set in
motion the development of the New England Episcopal
preparatory school. Muhlenberg also founded the Church of
the Holy Communion in New York to provide a place where
Communion would be offered each week, one of the first to

do so, and the first to offer free pews. He added vested choirs and Christmas greens, the Daily Office, and the observance of Holy Week. But his vision was not simply liturgical. He created a "fresh air" fund to send city children to the country in the summer, an employment agency for poor women, and a parish infirmary and dispensary. He was the founder of St. Luke's Hospital and founded a women's order that eventually led to the establishment of the Community of St. Mary, the oldest women's monastic order in the Episcopal Church. But more than all this, it was Muhlenberg who made the proposal that eventually led to the so-called Chicago-Lambeth Quadrilateral, a statement adopted by the Bishops of the Episcopal Church in 1886 and by the Bishops of the Anglican Communion in 1888. This statement proposed that the separated Christian churches should be united around four basic principles: the Bible, the two sacraments of baptism and Holy Communion, the creeds, and an apostolic ministry. That proposal is printed today in the back of the Prayer Book (pp. 876–78) among the historic documents of the church. Eventually the entire Anglican Communion endorsed the idea. But Muhlenberg's first proposal was even simpler. He proposed that the Episcopal Church simply offer to ordain bishops to serve in other churches. The Episcopal Church, as such, would have been unchanged, but gradually a common ministry shared throughout the churches would have been developed. He took episcopacy seriously as that which links us to the early church and gives us unity. If we shared that gift with other churches, he believed, the bishops would provide a link not only across time but also across the borders of denominationalism. His proposal, he said, was the "emancipation" of the episcopate. It is still a daring idea and at the center of current proposals for greater unity among the churches.

NINETEENTH-CENTURY WITNESS AND MISSION

As the nineteenth century wore on, Episcopal missionaries extended their work to the Far East and Africa. There are remarkable stories to be told. Samuel Isaac Joseph Scherechewsky, born of Jewish parents in Lithuania, came into the Episcopal Church as a young man and became a bishop in China and a translator of the Bible into Chinese. James Theodore Holly, born of African-American parents in Baltimore and brought up as a Roman Catholic, became a bishop of the Episcopal Church and established in Haiti a church that is equal in size today to the largest American dioceses and plays a central role in the life of that country.

In many other parts of the world, missionaries of the American Episcopal Church worked closely with English and Canadian missionaries, not to establish a colonial dependency of the Episcopal Church or Church of England, but to establish new national churches. And these new churches naturally thought of themselves not as English or American but simply as the catholic church in a new place. The Church in China called itself the Chung Hua Sheng Kung Hui, the Holy Catholic Church in China, and in Japan the Nippon Sei Ko Kai, the Holy Catholic Church in Japan. In Mexico and the Philippines, churches that had broken with Rome turned to the Episcopal Church for help in establishing national catholic churches without an English heritage. Within the space of a century, the Church of England had gone from being a unique national church to being the mother church of a worldwide family of churches with a common pattern of worship and episcopal ministry.

A CHANGING IMAGE

The other part of the story of the nineteenth century is the story of the maturing and development of the church itself.

The church that came to this country might be described as a
church still suffering from post-Reformation depression. It
was clearer in some ways about what it was not than about
what it was. An enormous catalyst in the development of a
new consciousness was the Oxford Movement, which began in
England in the early nineteenth century and set out to reawak-
en the English church to its catholic heritage. It is often
assumed that the Episcopal Church's awareness of its catholic
heritage is a result of the Oxford Movement, but the early
leaders of that movement were directly influenced by
American church leaders like John Henry Hobart. Hobart, in
turn, reflects the New England experience, which had helped
make church members aware of their catholic heritage.
Hobart's writings were known in England, and John Henry
Newman, one of the best known of the Oxford leaders,
acknowledged Hobart's influence on his thought. Hobart had
also traveled in England and met Newman and others of the
Oxford leaders. So the Episcopal Church helped shape the
Oxford Movement and the Oxford Movement in turn helped
shape the American Episcopal Church.

Nonetheless, a storm of controversy was raised in this country when English priests published a series of tracts that laid
stress on the catholic nature of Anglican Christianity. A rising
tide of immigration from southern Europe was making some
Americans fearful of what seemed like "alien influence," and
the Oxford tracts seemed to some to suggest similar influences
at work in the Episcopal Church. Students at General
Seminary were investigated by the House of Bishops amid
charges that the laws and traditions of the church were being
violated by new ceremonies such as bowing or genuflecting.
But the American church, thanks to its New England experience, had always had a sense of itself as catholic, and the oppo-
sition in this country never represented a majority of the

church. The new teaching and practice were controversial but they were supported by leading bishops and never condemned by the General Convention.

What may be hardest to understand, looking back, is the controversy caused as the new teaching began to express itself ceremonially. High churchmanship (a "high" emphasis on the importance of church and sacraments) was a doctrine, first of all, but it naturally found expression in ceremonial changes. If sacraments are important, that importance is expressed by the use of appropriate ceremony. But ceremonial expression often looked like what Roman Catholics do and non–Roman Catholic Christians were still fearful of what that might mean. Controversy raged for many years about clergy who wore chasubles and choirs that were vested and about the use of candles and crosses. Though these are common today in churches of almost every denomination, they were unfamiliar in the nineteenth century. In 1868 a canon was proposed to General Convention that would have prohibited any vestments except a surplice and stole or preaching bands and gown; banned also would have been the use of candles and crucifixes on the altar, bowing except during the Creed, the sign of the cross except in baptism, the elevation of the host, incense, and processions. There was prolonged and heated debate, but no such canon was ever passed.

The misnamed "Ritualist" controversy (it had to do primarily with ceremonial actions, but ritual is words) absorbed enormous energy in the latter half of the nineteenth century. But the controversy had to do, of course, with much more than the ceremonial. What was at stake was the life of the church, which needed to be enriched if the church was to be able to minister effectively to an increasingly diverse and changing country. Intellectual sermons were not going to reach new immigrants who barely spoke English or blue-collar workers who appreciated not only the color and sensual appeal of catholic liturgy but also a church that could bring its corporate life to bear on social problems.

It was natural that the impact of the Oxford Movement in this country would find expression not only in ceremonial but also in social action. The last part of the century was a time of enormous migration from Europe to America and from the countryside into the growing cities. The Industrial Revolution was changing the face of America, and the country had no laws to protect those who were caught up in the transformation. Leaders like Muhlenberg had already shown the church's concern for the situation, but in the latter part of the century one of the great leaders was William Rainsford, rector of St. George's, Stuyvesant Square, Manhattan. What had once been a large and wealthy church was nearly empty when he was called there, but before long he had made it a hive of activity. With the rector, four assistants, three deaconesses, and numerous lay volunteers to lead the work, organizations were created for almost everyone: a boys' club, a trade school, a Cadet Battalion, the Girls' Friendly Society, the Daughters of the King, a men's club, a group for married women, a Poor Fund, a grocery department, a Women's Industrial Exchange, a house in the country for those in need of "fresh air," and a trained nurse to call on and care for the sick. A six-story parish hall was built with classrooms for a church school of three thousand students and teachers and with a fully equipped gymnasium. Rainsford, in effect, invented the parish hall that we now take for granted.

But the development of the church's social mission can hardly be understood without noticing the changes in society that made such a mission increasingly important and at the same time provided new sources of leadership for the ministry that was needed. A growing mercantile and industrial society

was drawing people away from the farms and attracting a flow
of immigrants from Europe. Cities were growing and providing a rich life for some and hardship and poverty for others. It
was the women who were freed from the work of the farms
and cottage industries of an earlier society who were most
aware of the women and children working in sweatshops and
for whom society provided no health care or education. It was
the wealthier women and those of the growing middle class
who made possible the great social programs of the urban
churches. Some were paid (poorly) but most were volunteers.
Some also began to serve as nuns and deaconesses in newly re-
created ministries for women. These social action programs
were a vital training ground for the leadership of the developing women's movement within the church. To coordinate
these varied activities at the national level, the Women's
Auxiliary was organized in 1871 and gradually became a vital
support for the social and missionary outreach of the
Episcopal Church. It was the women of the church, in large
part, who raised its awareness of the need for mission and outreach and provided a major portion of the funding and personnel to do the work.

The structures of the church were also evolving to keep
pace with a fast-changing world. A church that had developed
first as a league of parishes and then as a federation of dioceses
began to find itself living like a national church. The creation
of the Domestic and Foreign Mission Society in 1835 had led
to the establishment of a Board of Missions and then, later in
the century, a General Board of Religious Education and a
Joint Commission on Social Service. Each of these was related
to the General Convention but otherwise acted independently
with its own officers and sources of financial support.

The need for closer cooperation and better funding led the
General Convention of 1919 to direct "the Presiding Bishop

and Council to administer and carry on the missionary, educational, and social work of the Church, of which work the Presiding Bishop shall be the executive head." Reflecting the rise of corporate America, the church, too, was now a corporation with a chief executive and departments to promote its products. But the corporate model, like any model, has its problems, and the church has never been entirely comfortable with a strong bureaucracy in its national headquarters in New York. From time to time the staff has been cut back and reorganized, but still there seems to be a need for some such structure. And so it continues to exist and to serve the church in whatever ways the church asks to be served.

The story of the Episcopal Church in the first half of the twentieth century is summed up best in the story of one man, Charles Henry Brent, whose life was woven into every aspect of the church's mission and witness in those years. Born and ordained in Canada, he came to the United States to serve in the church's inner-city work in Boston. Elected to serve as missionary bishop in the Philippines in 1901, he focused the church's work in the pagan north and Moslem south rather than in the cities and other areas where the Roman Catholic Church was already established. The opium trade was one of the great evils in Asia at the time, and Brent began an international crusade against it, representing the United States on the League of Nations Narcotics Committee. His vision of international and interchurch cooperation led to a major step forward in the ecumenical movement in 1927, through the calling of the first World Conference on Faith and Order, a conference over which he presided. Somehow he also found time to serve as a chaplain with American forces in World War I and, after the war, as bishop of Western New York, and even to write prayers that are included in the current Book of Common Prayer. Social witness, foreign mission, ecumenical cooperation, and prayer are the characteristics of the church at its best. Brent was unique in being personally involved in all of them, but he represented a church that, through the greater part of the twentieth century, was providing leadership in all these areas.

INTO THE NEW MILLENNIUM

By the beginning of the twentieth century, a church that many thought was so identified with England that it could not survive the Revolution had become so integral a part of American life that some began to think of it as the leading American church—even as a church that could become a unifying force for American Christians. In fact, although the Episcopal Church was still growing in numbers during the first part of the twentieth century, other churches were beginning to play a larger role also. The Roman Catholic Church, for one, was moving out from its ministry to new immigrants to become, like its members, a confident participant in American life. At the same time, Methodists and Presbyterians who had been divided between north and south were reuniting as national churches, and vigorous evangelical churches were beginning to find a national voice especially in the south and west. Furthermore, the social institutions the church had founded were being replaced by governmental and independent agencies and the energy of the churches was increasingly occupied in internal matters.

These were the years in which the Episcopal Church became for the first time truly a national church rather than a collection of dioceses without much common sense of purpose. In 1946 the church chose its first full-time national leader. Henry Knox Sherrill, the bishop of Massachusetts, was elected Presiding Bishop and resigned his diocese to give his whole attention to providing national leadership. Going on the radio to speak to the whole church, he called Episcopalians to work together and pray together. Determined to lead the way toward a greater unity among American Christians, Sherrill served as the first president of the National Council of Churches and later as president of the World Council of Churches.

The rapid growth of suburbs in the middle of the century led to a massive wave of church and parish hall construction and a strong emphasis on Christian education. But the boom was short-lived and the church found itself caught up first in the tensions of the civil rights movement, then in the movement to ordain women to the priesthood and episcopate, and the revision of the Prayer Book.

The generation of women who welcomed home the soldiers after World War II and went off to chauffeur children to school and Little League and piano lessons was quickly followed by a generation of women who wanted to shape careers for themselves outside the home. Volunteer roles in the church's life, while they had been an excellent preparation for a larger role, were no longer adequate. Once change began, it came rapidly. In first one diocese and then another, women began to serve on vestries, and in 1970 the first women began to serve as delegates to General Convention. A mere six years later, in 1976, the Convention voted to admit women to the priesthood and hundreds began to serve as priests throughout the country. Such change was not easily accepted. Here and there parishes broke away to form "continuing churches" of various sorts, and several dioceses resisted the ordination of women for many years. But the "continuing churches" could not agree among themselves as to what it was they stood for, and the bishops who dissented were gradually replaced by bishops who accepted women as priests. By 1988, Barbara Harris had been elected as Suffragan Bishop in Massachusetts, and not long after that other women were elected diocesan bishops in Vermont, Indianapolis, Utah, and Rhode Island.

All these events took place in the context of a society going through massive change and turmoil. Many Episcopalians saw only what was happening within the church and blamed the turmoil and declining numbers on the new Prayer Book adopted in 1979 and on the recognition of women as priests. But other mainline churches also were declining in numbers as the baby boom generation grew up and women found careers outside the home. The church became less significant as a place to educate children and provide women with a center for volunteer ministry. Less obvious was the way a changing church was attracting a new and far more diverse membership. Protestants searching for a church with a deeper sense of tradition and the mystery of worship as well as Roman Catholics looking for a church with more willingness to allow for independent thinking were finding a home in the Episcopal Church in increasing numbers. At the same time, the Episcopal Church's strong presence in the inner city and its long commitment to social involvement was drawing more Black Americans and members of the burgeoning Hispanic population. By 1982, it was estimated that almost 60 percent of the members of the Episcopal Church had been brought up outside its doors. The long decline in membership from the mid-60s to the mid-80s had also been halted and indeed reversed. The church, though still arguing angrily about sexuality and liturgical change, had begun again to think about the future of American Christianity in creative ways.

Controversy is often unpleasant, but it is a sign of life; a peaceful church would be one that was slowly dying. The church might have survived, as grand opera survives: deeply loved by a few but ignored by most. Instead, the church has attempted not only to preserve what is timeless but also to share it by reaching out in new and creative ways to the whole of society.

Indeed, the church at the beginning of the new millennium is a church ministering to a society in which change and diversity have become a way of life. The church, as it should,

reflects that diversity. In recent years a new seminary has been
founded in Pittsburgh to give better expression to the evangelical tradition in the church. One diocese has congregations
worshiping in fourteen different languages every Sunday. In
this American daughter church of the Church of England,
English is no longer spoken everywhere and members of
English ancestry are becoming a minority group. The United
States is a country changing more rapidly than ever, becoming
a society in which men and women have equal career opportunities and in which Black, Latino, and Asian Americans are
moving into the mainstream in significant numbers. America
is becoming what it has long promised it would be: a radically new kind of society, an international neighborhood in a
world community. A church whose primary boast is faithfulness to tradition will inevitably be shaken by the effort to minister to such a society, but a church without strong traditions
is likely to be torn apart by the stress and storm of change.

   But beneath the diversity, and hardly noticed, is a growing unity in the things that matter. The Eucharist is now the
main service every week in most parishes, and the ceremonies with which it is celebrated are much more similar
from one church to another than they were a generation ago.
Without drawing back at all from social ministry and witness, the church gives evidence of a deeper spiritual life, not
least in the election of a new Presiding Bishop, Frank Griswold,
who has centered his ministry on worship and prayer and spiritual growth. The third millennium of Christianity will present
new and greater challenges to the church, but an apostolic heritage combined with a taste for freedom and a willingness to
explore new forms of ministry provide the Episcopal Church
with tools that have served well in the past and are likely to do
so in the future.

QUESTIONS FOR FURTHER
THOUGHT AND DISCUSSION:

1. How much of the history discussed in this chapter was new information to you? Was your view of the Episcopal Church changed by what you learned? If so, in what ways? What topic did you find most enlightening or interesting? Why?

2. Do you agree with this statement on page 10: "Episcopal bishops may wear vestments that make them look authoritative, but they function in a much more collegial manner than do bishops in other traditions"? What kind of a role do you think bishops should play in the life of the local church?

3. Were you aware of the controversy regarding "high church" that is described on page 16? What is your personal preference for the style of worship? Why?

4. The Episcopal Church has a history of involvement in social and political issues, yet it exists in a country that values the separation of church and state. How do you think Christians can be most effective in working for social justice?

Worship

WHAT IS WORSHIP?

Toward the end of the Book of Revelation, the author describes two visions of things to come: one is a vision of heaven in which there are "flashes of lightning, rumblings, peals of thunder, and a violent earthquake" (16:18), and the other is a vision of a new earth in which God will dwell and will "wipe away every tear" from human eyes (21:3–4). In the biblical vision, God is the unknown and unknowable and, at the same time, an intimate personal friend. Both are true, yet how both can be true at the same time remains a mystery. At the heart of the Christian experience of God there is a mystery, and the only possible response to such a mystery is worship.

Worship is the response of the created and limited human mind and heart to the unlimited Creator, who is sensed but never fully known. Worship is a response to beauty, to love, to human need, to our deepest fears, to our greatest joys. It enlists all that is best and most creative in the human spirit. It involves language, music, art, and dance, and sound and sight and smell and touch and taste. Corporate worship brings us together in common action with many others, yet we also have a need sometimes to separate ourselves from others in order to worship. We worship because we are human, not divine. Worship fulfills our human nature by drawing us closer to God.

For more than two thousand years Christians have worshiped God in many ways, from the rich solemnity of the Orthodox Church with its golden icons and clouds of incense to the simple austerity of the Quaker meeting house with no altar or stained glass or cross or candles. Although worship in the Episcopal Church does not normally reach those extremes, it can vary considerably from one faith community to another. Yet beneath the surface differences, there is a common concern for order and a desire to offer back to God as many of God's gifts as possible.

THE BUILDING

Worship can and does take place everywhere: in soaring cathedrals and tiny chapels, in a clearing in the woods, beside a sickbed, in a prison chapel, around a kitchen table. We worship when we say grace at meals and when we kneel beside our beds at night. But the central act of Christian worship takes place week by week in parish churches, and they also vary widely. You can visit the Cathedral of St. John the Divine in New York City and learn that it has a center aisle a tenth of a mile long and that it is larger than any other Gothic cathedral in the world. There are Episcopal churches with white spires like those of a New England meeting house and Episcopal churches that look like Greek temples, and there are modern Episcopal churches that are round with an altar in the center. The simplest definition of a church is "an altar with a roof over it." Whatever the shape of the church, that definition will probably work. A church is a building designed to allow Christian people to gather around an altar for a common meal.

But churches serve other purposes, too. Christians gather for instruction as well as Communion, so they need a place from which lessons may be read and sermons given. Perhaps there will be two places; a lectern for the readings and a pulpit for the sermon. But no building design can locate both a pulpit and an altar so that each is the focal point. There are colonial churches in which the pulpit dominates the church and the altar is a small table below it. Such churches were built at a time when the sermon was the center of worship and Communion was held only on occasion. There are modern churches in which the altar is central and the pulpit is a movable reading desk. That reflects a different sense of priorities. Many Episcopal churches were built under the influence of the Gothic revival in the nineteenth century when people believed that every church should look like an English cathedral with a large rectangular area, the nave, for people to sit in, a smaller rectangular area for the choir, and a still smaller area, the sanctuary, for the altar. It's a building design that reflects a class-structured society with each order in its proper place and God at a safe distance, yet it also provides a sense of mystery that is appropriate in any act of worship of a limitless God by very limited human beings. Many of these buildings have been redesigned in recent years to bring the altar forward and allow a closer relationship between those at the altar and those in the congregation. This, too, is appropriate since God has come near to us in Jesus Christ, yet the sense of mystery is inevitably diminished by such change. Every church building is the result of current emphases and certain compromises. How, after all, would the author of the Book of Revelation design a church for the God whose throne is surrounded by thunder and lightning yet who comes near to us to dry our tears?

THE PRAYER BOOK

Worship in the Episcopal Church is shaped not only by the buildings we make or inherit (and which we often reshape) but also by the books we use (and also reshape). Many other churches provide only a hymnal and print a new order of service each week. When you take your seat in an Episcopal Church, you will almost certainly find two books near at hand, most often in a pew rack. One is a Book of Common Prayer, and the other is a hymnal. In many churches there is also a Bible, but you can usually participate in a service without looking at the Bible and perhaps without using the hymnal. You cannot, however, unless you have memorized it, take part in the service without using the Book of Common Prayer. Nothing is more central to the life of the Episcopal Church than worship using that book. Other churches may find their unity in an organizational system or a set of beliefs, but Episcopalians find their unity first of all in worship using the Book of Common Prayer. We have noticed already how, at the time of the Reformation, while Christians in most of Europe were defining their positions by drawing up statements of belief, the Church of England issued instead a Prayer Book. "Heretofore," said the preface to the First English Prayer Book, "there has been great diversity in saying and singing in churches within this realm," but now "all the realm shall have but one use." Obviously there would still be great differences between the services of the great cathedrals with their staffs of clergy and choirs and the services in a small country church with one priest and a few people, but the words and the order of worship would be the same. So, too, after the American Revolution, although there were great differences between the churches in the south and those in New England, one of the first orders of business was to adopt a Book of Common Prayer. Episcopalians would find their unity in worship.

If you open the Prayer Book, you will find a table of contents and a preface and then a statement about "the Service of the Church." It tells us that the Holy Eucharist is the "principal act of Christian worship on the Lord's Day" and that there are other services also that are "appointed for public worship." It goes on to say a few things about the roles played in worship by bishops, priests, deacons, and lay people, and about the use of music. Obviously worship in the Episcopal Church is not just a matter of a preacher and congregation, a few prayers and some hymns. There is a pattern that involves a variety of people taking part in a "liturgy," an action that involves everyone who attends.

We come then to a series of pages that provide an outline for the services of "the Church Year." We see reference to changing seasons and saints' days. Not until page 37 do we come to the first services, and these are services planned for daily use. This is a church that wants us to know right away that worship cannot be confined to Sundays. Turning pages rapidly, we find services of Morning and Evening Prayer in traditional and contemporary language and then "Daily Devotions" for individuals and families. Prayer is to be offered not only at church but at home or wherever we are. After that we find more than a hundred pages of prayers called "collects," the theme prayers for each Sunday and Holy Day of the year, and then almost fifty pages of services for Lent and Holy Week.

One-third of the way through the book we come to the service that might logically have come first, the service of Holy Baptism. The Prayer Book, though, is designed in such a way that the services most used, Baptism and the Eucharist, come near the center. It's easier to hold a book open at the middle, and the Prayer Book is structured with an eye to convenience.

Turn further pages and you find yourself in a series of life-changing events: marriage, "Thanksgiving for the Birth or Adoption of a Child," "The Reconciliation of a Penitent," prayers for a ministry to the sick and at the time of death, and then the Burial Office. Now we have looked quickly over the changing seasons of the year and the changing circumstances of life, and we are only half way through the book. Here we come to the services that provide for the three ordained ministries: bishops, priests, and deacons, and then for the celebration of a new ministry and the consecration of a church. These may be rare events in our ordinary experience, but we begin to sense that this book intends to be complete, to provide for the whole of life in a carefully thought-out way.

Now comes a surprise: one complete book of the Bible: the Book of Psalms, the ancient hymnal of the Jewish people. But what form of prayer is more familiar than the Twenty-third Psalm, "The LORD is my shepherd"? And what collection of prayers or hymns sums up the whole of human life, its joy and thankfulness, its sorrows and doubts, or brings us back so often to the source of our comfort and strength, in language as familiar and helpful as that of the psalms?

If you are still turning pages, you will come, on page 810, to a collection of prayers for a variety of purposes including such especially useful ones as "Before Receiving Communion," and "After Receiving Communion," and "Grace at Meals."

We're almost at the end, and here we find an outline of the Christian faith as the Episcopal Church teaches it and then some historic documents of Christian history, summaries of the church's teaching that still guide us. We end as we began with tables for finding Holy Days and with suggested readings to be used on the Sundays of the year and for daily use as well.

Here in one book is the whole of life and answers to most of our questions about the church. No wonder Episcopalians are as likely to have a Prayer Book by their bed as a Bible. And this is simply the latest version of a book first published in 1549, the first Prayer Book ever in the English language. It's a book that has been around for a while, that sums up a lot of experience, that gives us the same prayers to say that saints and sinners alike have recited over the centuries. A similar book can be found in the churches of the Anglican Communion all around the world. As we become familiar with this book, we become familiar with a pattern of worship that unites us to Christians in every age and every part of the world.

THE EUCHARIST

At the center of the Book of Common Prayer is the service called The Holy Eucharist. In earlier editions of the Prayer Book it was called the Mass or the Lord's Supper or the Holy Communion. Eucharist, the common name today, comes from the word used in the Bible to describe what Jesus did at the Last Supper. He took bread and gave thanks. Even today, Greek-speaking people use that word "eucharist" to say thank you. So this is a service in which Christians come together to give God thanks, to remember that all we have is a gift, and to offer praise and thanksgiving for God's goodness.

The first Christians called it "the breaking of the bread" because it was as Jesus broke bread with the disciples that they recognized his presence with them. In those days the meal was probably more like a potluck supper than a solemn ritual. But as time went by, it became impractical to arrange for a full meal for all the church members every week, and the sharing of the bread and wine became a separate action with prayers that took a more and more set form. By the middle of the second century we find records of prayers that are still familiar: "Lift up your hearts; We lift them to the Lord," for example, and "Lord, have mercy."

The pattern of worship that finally developed in those early centuries was actually two services put together. Still today, the Eucharist has two clearly separate parts. We begin with a service centered on the reading of God's word and instruction. This has its origins in the Jewish synagogue service in which Jesus and the early disciples frequently took part. We read from the Scriptures the story of what God has done among us and we are asked to consider how that is related to our own lives. The second part of the service is centered on the bread and wine at the altar. We offer these gifts, give thanks for them, break the bread, and come to receive Communion. The Gospels tell how Jesus did those same four things with his disciples: "He took bread, and when he had given thanks, he broke it, and gave it to his disciples." If the first part of the service is primarily words, the second part is primarily action; through both God is always at work in our lives.

One of the greatest tragedies of Christian history is that when the Reformation erupted in the sixteenth century, the Eucharist lost its centrality in Christian worship. The reformers made an effort to restore the Eucharist as a common meal in which Christians shared God's gifts, but there were so many disagreements among them as to exactly what happened in the service that they became divided not only from the papacy but also from each other. Confusion about the meaning of the Eucharist combined with excitement over the new availability of the Bible in the common language led some Protestant churches to relegate the Eucharist to a secondary role.

Medieval theologians had used a good deal of ingenuity in trying to explain exactly what it is that happens when the bread and wine are offered and blessed. The bread and wine, they agreed, become the body and blood of Christ, but how does this happen? They concentrated on the words Jesus spoke at the Last Supper, and they agreed that when those words were said by the priest, the bread and wine are transformed into the body and blood of Christ. The reformers did not doubt that Christians were united with Christ in some way in this service, but in their effort to reduce the power of the church over people's lives they were uncomfortable with an approach that concentrated so much power in the priesthood. Some reformers thought Christ's presence was in response to the faith of the believer, while others saw the Lord's Supper as a meal in which Christ was simply remembered. The Church in England was influenced by all the continental reformers but maintained the belief, in common with Luther, that the bread and wine did truly become the body and blood of Christ. Queen Elizabeth perhaps said it best when she summed up her belief in a simple poem:

> He was the Word that spake it;
> He took the bread and brake it;
> And what his word did make it,
> That I believe and take it.

Theories, in other words, are all very well, but finally it is facts that matter. How Christ comes to us in the Eucharist is far less important than the fact that when we receive the bread and wine, Christ truly comes into our lives. Over the centuries, Episcopalians have expressed this central truth in many ways. Sometimes the priest has stood alone at a high altar with his back to the congregation, enveloped in clouds of incense, and communicants, walking up a long aisle to kneel at the altar rail, have known the mystery of the presence in human lives of a God beyond knowing. Sometimes, on the other hand, the priest has stood at a simple table, facing the congregation, and with clergy and lay people standing around the altar passing the bread and wine around the circle, communicants have known the love that comes into our lives in simple and familiar things.

The Book of Common Prayer provides the framework for this to happen. Very little is said about vestments or outward embellishment. It is inevitable and appropriate that this should vary from place to place. Whether there are two candles on the altar or many or none is a matter to be decided locally. "Unity in essentials; freedom in non-essentials" is a traditional

Anglican pattern. The common life of the church should be
orderly but not regimented.

SACRAMENTS

No one service or way of worship can contain the whole
mystery, but whether the Eucharist is elaborate or simple,
bread and wine are at the center as a sign of God's presence.
Material things become a means of conveying a reality beyond
the physical world. So, too, in other rituals of the church, outward signs are used as the means by which God acts in our
lives. We speak of these as sacraments. The Catechism defines
a sacrament as "an outward and visible sign of an inward and
spiritual grace given to us." Sacramental worship is worship
that makes us aware of God's gifts and recognizes the Divine
presence in the created world.

At the center of the pattern of worship in the Episcopal
Church is a sacramental understanding of God's relationship
with this world: that God can and does work through material things to change human lives. The Bible itself shows us God
working in and through material things, first in making the
world and then, most importantly, by coming into the world
in a human body to show us what God's love looks like in
human flesh. Human beings have misused created things so
often that some forms of religion, even some forms of
Christianity, are inclined to distrust and reject created things
as inherently evil. But the problem is in our misuse of them,
not in the things themselves. Sacramental worship recognizes
the inherent goodness of all God's gifts and uses them freely,
offering the best we have in acts of worship. The use of candles
and flowers and vestments and incense are all expressions of
this sacramental approach.

So, also, are the ways that Episcopalians use their bodies in
their worship, standing and sitting and kneeling, moving up to
the altar and back again, joining in processions around the

church and even around the neighborhood. The story is told of an old sea captain who happened to come into an Episcopal Church one day. When friends asked him afterwards about his experience, he answered, "I was out at sea at first, but then I just put down my anchor and rose and fell with the tide." The use of our bodies in the movements of the service is a result of our belief that God has used material things to communicate with us and that we can use them to communicate with God. Christmas celebrates the fact that God came into this world in a human body; Good Friday tells us how serious was that commitment to human flesh and experience; Easter and Ascension Day tell us that God continues to value the human body, raising it from death to eternal life.

Sacramental worship reflects this understanding of the meaning of the gospel. This is the fundamental reason for standing and sitting and kneeling. It is a way of participating in worship with our bodies as well as our hearts and minds. So it is that visitors to an Episcopal Church will also notice that some people sign themselves with the cross at certain points in the service and that some genuflect (kneel briefly on one knee) when entering or leaving their pews and that many will bow their heads at the name of Jesus and when a cross passes by in procession. All these are ways of involving our bodies in our worship. There are no rules to govern this kind of conduct; it is a matter of what individuals find helpful. But outward expression of this kind is as natural as using our bodies to express our love for others. Two people in love can sit at opposite ends of a couch and gaze soulfully into each other's eyes, but sooner or later most people find it helpful to get closer and to use their bodies to say what their words can never fully express. "Platonic relationships" are inadequate.

For very similar reasons, the Prayer Book suggests that a celebration of the Eucharist ought to involve a variety of people. The service is not a performance by the priest watched by the people or even something the priest does that enables the people to go to the altar to get their communion. It was a basic principle of the Reformation (as it was fundamental to the life of the early church), that all should participate in the Eucharist in some way. The first English Prayer Book specified that there could be no service unless two or three had indicated to the priest that they would receive communion that day. There was to be no "priest's mass" said by a priest with no congregation, since that would be contrary to the very meaning and nature of the service. A corporate action requires the presence of the body. The Eucharist is a corporate activity by all the members. At the very least, all join in certain prayers and all make certain responses. But better still, some will be assigned to act as readers and another will lead the intercessions and still others will be ushers and acolytes and assist with the ministration of Communion. The service should be a corporate activity in which all the members of the body work together.

This shared, common life begins at baptism, which in recent years has been regaining its central place in the church's life. The first English Prayer Book gave instructions that baptisms should be held on Sundays and Holy Days when most people could be present so that all might be reminded of the promises they made or that were made for them when they were baptized. This was something too important to the church's life to be done in a quiet corner. Unfortunately, as the years went by, it became common practice for baptisms to be held privately on a Sunday afternoon with the priest and family members gathered around the font. That practice now has nearly disappeared and baptisms are held again as they should be, when the whole congregation is present.

More often also in recent years, adult baptisms have been celebrated openly and publicly and with lengthy and careful preparation. In the early church, candidates for baptism were admitted as "catechumens" and instructed carefully before they were baptized. The final period of preparation took place in the forty days before Easter. The baptisms were then performed on Easter Eve so that the new church members could receive communion for the first time on Easter Day. This practice, too, is becoming more common as the church finds itself again a missionary community in a basically pagan society and attempts to prepare new members carefully for their role as witnesses to the risen Christ.

There has been much controversy as to the definition of a sacrament in the history of the church, and there is no generally accepted list. St. Augustine spoke of salt and ashes, the Creed, the Lord's Prayer, and the baptismal font as sacraments. In the late Middle Ages, theologians came to believe that there were seven sacraments, but the Roman Catholic Church adopted this view officially only after the Reformation. The 1979 Prayer Book tells us that there are "two great sacraments of the Gospel," Baptism and the Holy Eucharist, and five other "sacramental rites… confirmation, ordination, holy matrimony, reconciliation of a penitent, and unction." Debate continues over the relationship between confirmation and baptism, but unction or the anointing of the sick (never confined to "last rites" in the Episcopal Church) has become widely used in recent years. Sacramental confession has been less widely used in the Episcopal Church than the Roman Catholic, perhaps because there is a General confession of sins in almost every principal service, but any Episcopal priest will hear a confession "anytime and anywhere" (Prayer Book, p. 446).

THE DAILY OFFICE

While the Eucharist is the chief service on Sundays and the other sacraments mark special occasions, the Daily Offices of Morning and Evening Prayer are intended to provide a

framework for daily life. The ancient monastic orders had
been dissolved by the time the first Prayer Book was published,
but the pattern of monastic life with its seven daily times of
prayer had left a deep imprint on English society. A primary
object of the first English Prayer Book was to make prayer as
much as possible a part of daily life for everyone by combining
the seven monastic offices into two for both priests and people.

Although the ideal of participation in daily prayer by all
church members has never been realized, the possibility is
increased because the daily offices can be said by an individual
at home or in a commuter train. There is no better way to take
part in the continual offering of prayer and praise to God that
is the church's primary work.

The 1979 Book of Common Prayer makes a new effort to
encourage daily prayer by providing much shorter orders of
service for morning, noonday, early evening, and evening.
One of these services can be said in well under two minutes;
even with a period of silence and some individual prayers they
could be said in less than five minutes. It is quite possible to
imagine these services becoming a familiar part of the life of
every Episcopalian and the biblical image of the church as a
people of prayer (see, for example, Ephesians 6:18, Philippians
4:6, Colossians 4:2) being realized at last. Worship is too
important to Episcopalians to leave it to the clergy. It is worship that makes this church what it is.

MUSIC

Any discussion of worship in the Episcopal Church would
be incomplete without some mention of music. It has been
said that "the Christian liturgy was born singing and has never
ceased to sing."[1] The Gospels tell us that Jesus and his disciples
ended the last supper by singing a hymn (Mark 14:26). We
read of Paul singing in prison (Acts 16:25) and the epistles

speak frequently of singing (Romans 15:9; 1 Corinthians
14:15, 26; Ephesians 5:19; Colossians 3:16) as does the Book
of Revelation (4:8, 10; 5:9, 12, 13; 7:12; 11:17; 14:3; 15:3).
The Book of Revelation even tells us that the Sanctus (Holy,
holy, holy) is sung in heaven (4:8) and that the saints there (a
useful example to some Episcopalians!) sing a "new hymn"
(5:9, 14:3).

Why is singing so important? The practical reasons are that
sung words carry better and more clearly than spoken words
and that voices stay in unison better in singing than in speaking. But music also adds expressiveness, especially joy, to the
words we speak. And music also expresses, better perhaps than
any other medium, the universality and inclusiveness of the
church. We no longer speak Latin, but we can still sing the
ancient plainsong melodies. Few of us speak German, but we
can sing Luther's great hymns. None of us has experienced
slavery, but we can sing the hymns created by African-
Americans during the years of slavery. An ordinary Sunday
morning in an Episcopal Church will find a congregation
singing hymn tunes from Ireland and Wales and Russia with
words from ancient Greece and medieval Spain. Many musi-
cians and others who love music have come into the Episcopal
Church primarily because of its music. God gave us the gift of
music, and in the Episcopal Church the great music of the
whole human race—from the simple plainsong of the Middle
Ages to the great organ music of recent centuries—is a familiar part of the offering of worship.

WORSHIP DEFINES THE CHURCH

Earlier in this chapter, a passing reference was made to the
historic documents at the end of the Prayer Book. One of
those documents is the Articles of Religion, an attempt made
by the Church of England in the midst of the controversies of

the Reformation to state a position on certain key issues. Article 19 attempts to say what the church is, and it does it in terms of worship: "The visible Church of Christ is a congregation of faithful men, in which the pure word of God is preached, and the Sacraments be duly ministered according to Christ's ordinance" (p. 871). The church, in other words, is people who worship God and are fed and formed in that place where Christ's death and resurrection are encountered and proclaimed. Though the particular expression has changed from time to time and from place to place, this understanding has remained central to the nature of the Episcopal Church.

QUESTIONS FOR FURTHER
THOUGHT AND DISCUSSION:

1. This chapter describes a variety of interpretations of exactly what happens in the Eucharist. What is your belief about
the bread and wine you receive in the Eucharist?

2. Page 39 lists a number of reasons that music is important
in worship. Can you think of any others? Is music an essential
part of worship for you? Why or why not?

3. Is the pattern of worship in your parish effective in drawing and keeping new members? If so, what aspects of worship
seem to be the most significant? If not, what do you think are
the reasons?

---

1. J. Gelineau, "Music and Singing in the Liturgy," *The Study of
Liturgy*, ed. C. Jones, G. Wainwright, E. Yarnold, and P. Bradshaw
(New York: Oxford University Press, 1992), p. 494.

The Bible in the Episcopal Church

THE BIBLE IN WORSHIP

On the first Easter Day, two of Jesus' disciples were walking sadly away from Jerusalem convinced that the Lord they loved was dead and buried. As they walked, Jesus approached them and walked with them, but they were so convinced he was dead that they failed to recognize him. So he talked with them about their recent experiences as they walked on, and "opened the Scriptures" to them to explain how all that they had experienced was necessary in God's plan. Toward the end of the day the disciples persuaded Jesus to stop with them and share a meal. As they did so, he took a loaf of bread, gave thanks to God, and broke the bread. Then they recognized him (Luke 24:13–35).

This story told by St. Luke should be familiar to Episcopalians not simply as a story but as their own experience. In our Christian journey, the Scriptures are of critical importance as a means of understanding God's nature and purpose; as we read and study them, Jesus walks with us and we grow in knowledge. And then, when we gather for a simple meal, we know Jesus' presence with us in the breaking of

43

the bread. Word and sacrament are the means by which God works in our lives to enlighten us and to be present with us.

Suppose you came to a service in the Episcopal Church for the first time. What would your impression be? Put aside, if you can, all the questions you might have about the ceremonies you saw and think just about the words of the service. Would it strike you that it was remarkable how much of the service was simply words recited from the Bible?

To begin with, there are usually four passages of Scripture, three lessons and a psalm. These lessons are selected according to a plan so that over three years almost all of the New Testament and a great deal of the Old Testament are read, and the Prayer Book provides a plan of daily services in which even more of the Bible is read. If Episcopalians attend services each Sunday and follow the sequence of daily readings, few other Christians can claim as rich and full an exposure to the Bible as they will have. No other church over the last four and one-half centuries has regularly given its members so much of the Bible in their own language.

Perhaps you would also notice during the service that the hymns, the choir anthem if there is one, and the prayers are based on the Bible. You would notice the story of the Last Supper (1 Corinthians 11:23–25), for example, in the middle of the Prayer of Consecration and the song Isaiah and St. John heard sung by angels, "Holy, holy, holy" (Isaiah 6:3, Revelation 4:8), at the beginning of that same prayer. There are references in the opening prayer, the Collect for Purity, to Matthew 6:6, John 16:8, John 16:13 and Romans 8:26–27. So, too, the blessing most often used at the end of the service, "The Peace of God which passes all understanding…" is based on Philippians 4:7. The eucharistic service is saturated with this kind of biblical reference. One-third of the Prayer Book is either a book of the Bible (the Psalms) or a guide to reading the Bible; the rest of the Prayer Book is based on the Bible and makes constant reference to it. The services of the Book of Common Prayer are a way of turning the Bible into prayer. ※ This is much less likely to happen in informal or spontaneous prayer since few people are so thoroughly familiar with the Scriptures that the right phrases for prayer come instinctively to their lips.

We have said that the life of the Episcopal Church is centered in worship, but that is not to say that the Episcopal Church is not deeply centered on the Bible. It is the Bible that forms and shapes our worship. The Bible in worship is not so much a book of instruction, nor simply God's word to us, but it becomes a language we learn with which we speak to God.

It is important, again, to notice that Episcopalians hear the Bible most often in church in an act of worship in the company of other Christians. The effect of that hearing is very different from what happens when we read the Bible alone in our room. We should, of course, do that also, but we begin the week by hearing the Bible in worship and with others. That should always be the place we start. Hearing the Bible first within the worshiping community has several consequences.

First, we are reminded of the limitations of all language. "What shall I say, my God, my holy joy?" asked one of the saints. What words are adequate to express either our needs or God's limitless glory? But worship enables us to go beyond language. We cannot find words adequate to God's glory, but we can sing and bow our heads and hold up our hands and "present... our selves, our souls and bodies, to be a reasonable, holy, and living sacrifice" (Prayer Book, p. 336, based on Romans 12:1). In worship we come to know God in a way beyond words. All words, even those of the Bible, are inadequate to express the fullness of God's love and power and glory. The words of the Bible, then, are seen as a reflection of what we have experienced more directly in worship. When the Bible says, "Who is so great a God as our God?" (Psalm 77:13), we know what it means because we have been involved in worship.

Second, we are reminded of the limitations of our own individual understanding. Everyone else in church will hear the words of the Bible from a different perspective from mine, and they will therefore hear different things than I will hear. It is appropriate that each of us should hear something different, but it is important for me to remember that what I hear is not the whole message or the only message. In my own room, I might come to believe that; in group Bible study and in church I am much less likely to see it that way. Because of our limitations, there is a danger that an individual could misinterpret Scripture and draw the wrong conclusions from it. The Anglican tradition, emphasizing corporate reading and hearing of Scripture, reminds us to bring our private thoughts, insights, and understandings into the community where the collective wisdom and faith can help us to understand and interpret Scripture with greater accuracy. We need then to study the Bible together and enrich our individual understanding by sharing our particular insights with others.

Third, the statements of the Bible, in the context of worship, gain a fullness and balance they might not otherwise have. A passage that sounds judgmental, for example, is heard differently if we are about to join in the Confession of Sin, receive Absolution, and then go the altar to receive Christ's life into ours; judgment is always balanced in the liturgy by mercy—and if the readings center on love, the Confession of Sin reminds us of the reality of judgment. Likewise, the single events of the life of Christ that we hear in the Gospel are heard in the context of a service in which we recall, always, his death and resurrection. Christ is not simply a teacher or healer; he died for us and rose again.

THE AUTHORITY OF THE BIBLE

The Prayer Book contains several statements on the central place of the Bible in our common life. Notice, for example, the way the church is defined on page 871 as a place where "the pure Word of God is preached, and the Sacraments [are] duly ministered;" Word and sacrament together make the church. Notice also the Catechism statements on pages 853–54 of the Prayer Book that define the nature of the Bible, the statement in the Articles of Religion (Article VI on page 868) about the sufficiency of the Holy Scriptures for salvation, and the statements made by the bishops of the Anglican Communion on page 877, which say that the Scriptures "as the rule and ultimate standard of faith" are the first prerequisite for Christian unity.

These statements are not mere theory; they are what we act out in our worship week by week and day by day. It is out of this experience of the Bible in worship that we come to understand the claims made for its authority.

The Bible itself says, for example, "All scripture is inspired by God and is useful for teaching, for reproof, for correction, and for training in righteousness" (1 Timothy 3:16). But "useful" leaves a great deal to the imagination, and Christians have imagined a variety of possibilities. At the time of the Reformation some maintained that Christians should do only what Scripture directly commanded, while others maintained that Christians could do anything except what the Scriptures prohibited. The first way would hardly permit you to get out of bed in the morning and brush your teeth, while the second path opens up wide fields of opportunity for those with vivid imaginations. Richard Hooker, at the end of the sixteenth century, noticed that some Christians claimed that the Scripture alone was not enough and other authority was needed, while others claimed that with the Scripture no other guidance was needed. The first opinion he rejected out of hand, but the second moved him to caution that we should be careful not to claim so much for Scripture that we make its valid claims unbelievable as well. The Anglican position, stated clearly in the service of ordination and elsewhere, is that we should require no beliefs except what we are persuaded can be solidly based on the Scriptures, but we are free to adopt beliefs and customs that seem consistent with the scriptural witness even though they may not be directly stated. There is, for example, no direct scriptural authority for worship on Sunday, for Altar Guilds, stained-glass windows, or church school programs, but the first day of the week or "Lord's Day" was significant to Christians from the earliest times (Acts 20:7, 1 Corinthians 16:2, Revelation 1:10), the adornment of worship, within reasonable limits, is consistent with the patterns of worship reflected in Exodus 38–39, 1 Kings 7, and Revelation 4, and the training of children is commended in Proverbs 22:6 and Ephesians 6:4.

But the Bible is not a set of instructions that can give us simple answers to all questions or a text with which to prove points. In the first place, the guidance the Bible gives was provided for a society very different from ours and still in the early stages of growth in knowledge of God's love. The existence of such instructions as to stone a disobedient son (Deuteronomy 21:18–21) should give us pause in simply quoting the Bible to justify our actions. Sometimes Jesus himself overrode scriptural commandments with new commands, as in the Sermon on the Mount (Matthew 5:21–48). So, when we find the Bible saying, "An eye for an eye and a tooth for tooth," we can read it as a bloodthirsty law to be ignored (which makes large parts of the Bible irrelevant), an unchanging standard to be enforced in our modern penal code (which puts us back to a pre-Christian world), or we can learn through further study that this command was a step forward for a world whose usual rule was unlimited vengeance (e.g., a life for an eye), and that it was a rule superseded in its turn by Jesus' injunction to turn the other cheek (Matthew 5:39).

In the second place, any set of words is open to various interpretations. When I write instructions to my computer, the computer will read those instructions and follow them exactly. Sometimes I will be frustrated because the computer does exactly what I told it to when I have not gotten my instructions exactly right. But there is never any difference between what I write and what the computer does. When a human being reads the Bible, on the other hand, the results are far less predictable. Even if the Bible were like computer instructions, a code to be followed exactly, the results would be unpredictable because human beings are not computers and not predictable at all. God, being ultimately responsible for both the text of the Bible and the nature of human beings, presumably understood that in creating both and made allowances. The authority of the Bible is not that of a dictator or rule book, and to understand it better, we need to think about what the Bible actually is.

WHAT THE BIBLE IS

Let's begin with some history. The Reformation took place because some Christians felt that the church had been giving them the wrong answers to their questions about the human relationship with God. Many Christians felt that they would do better to turn to the Bible for answers. Unfortunately, they were used to getting very specific directions for their lives from the church, and many began asking for the same sort of directions from the Bible. For example, the church had ordered Christians to fast on Friday, so it was natural to turn to the Bible for directions that might be different but would be just as simple and clear. Instead of looking for a different kind of authority, people looked for the same sort of authority from a different source. In effect, they asked the Bible to become their authority instead of asking whether Christians were supposed to have such authority at all. But since the Bible does not provide specific answers to many questions and human beings may read the same passages with very different understanding, this kind of use of the Bible has produced divisions in the church with many different denominations claiming the single true interpretation.

But the Bible is not a rule book. If God had wanted us to have a rule book, surely a better one could have been provided than this. The Bible is something quite different; we go to it not to find specific words to answer our questions but to find the Word who created us and knows our need before we ask.

The Bible is a collection of writings produced at various times and places over a span of more than a thousand years in which we can see what God has done through individuals and through the history of nations and peoples. It begins with the story of a primitive people who were slaves in Egypt and who knew themselves to have been set free through God's action in their history. God had acted to set them free; therefore God must be One who cared about freedom and who hated oppression. God, they began to see, was a God of justice. Later this same people became secure and wealthy and began to enslave others. Inspired men, called prophets, warned that God's justice was as likely to destroy them as the Egyptians if they persisted, and not long after that they found themselves defeated and carried off into Babylonian captivity. But then the prophets spoke of mercy and forgiveness, and indeed, the people were set free and were able to return to their own country and begin again. But the knowledge of God's care for them led them to dream of a peace and freedom beyond any they had yet experienced and to look for God to act again both in history and at the end of history. The Bible tells how God did act in Christ and how those who came to know and follow Christ continued to speak of God's purpose in history and beyond it.

So the Bible is, first of all, a record of what God has done in history, a God revealed in real events and supremely revealed in one real life. It is the story of how certain people came slowly to understand who God is by meditating on these actions of God in history. That aspect of the Bible alone gives us much to ponder. If God overthrew the Egyptians because they were unjust and if God's own people were sent into exile when they were unjust, how will God judge my society, my business, my personal life? If God is working in history toward a purpose, am I in my private life, in my church, and in my society working toward that purpose or against it? Read this way, the Bible may not always add to our comfort.

The Bible also, of course, tells us in the New Testament the story of Jesus: not simply a biography, but a gospel, good news, the story of a life that changes all life. If God is supremely revealed in the life of Jesus, have I come to know God in that life, in a living and personal relationship with God in Christ?

The Bible also contains the story of how the church began and shows us the problems it faced and how it dealt with them. Sometimes those problems are very similar to ours and sometimes very different. But even the way Christians dealt with issues different from those we face may be useful to us today. St. Paul, for example, wrote to the church in Corinth at great length about the problem of food offered to idols (1 Corinthians 8, 10:14–32). Should Christians eat such food or not? This is not a problem most of us face, but the guidance Paul offers remains as relevant as ever: eat the food or not, as you please, but give no offense to others and do all for the glory of God.

Sometimes, however, the guidance given may seem to be relevant to us when it is not. When St. Paul writes that women should keep their heads covered in church, he is applying a contemporary norm of decency and saying that Christian women should follow the contemporary norms. But in America today, decency no longer requires a head covering and it would be unnecessarily old-fashioned to make that a requirement. It is not the specific advice given that is relevant to us but the principle behind the advice. In a somewhat similar way, Episcopalians came to believe that when the Bible says women should not speak in church (1 Corinthians 14:33–36), it is again asking church members to follow contemporary etiquette, but when St. Paul says that in Christ there is neither male nor female, slave or free, but all are one in Christ Jesus (Galatians 3:28), he is holding up a vision of a very different society in which neither race nor gender is a barrier to church membership or leadership. Thus, when we come at last into a world in which women are truly free to use the gifts God has given them in any walk of life, the church should not only accept that change but rejoice in it and endorse it by its own practice. We would understand the Bible to be holding up a vision of a transformed society on the one hand, but on the other hand suggesting that we not move toward that vision in such a way that others are unnecessarily offended.

But the distinction between eternal principles and expedient practices is not always clear and will often be controversial. The Episcopal Church has been badly divided over the issue of ordaining women to the priesthood and it has been very difficult to find the right balance between responding in justice to those called to be ordained while respecting the consciences of those not convinced. One piece of guidance the Prayer Book gives is that "we understand the meaning of the Bible by the help of the Holy Spirit, who guides the Church in the interpretation of the Scriptures" (pp. 853–54). In other words, we should seek the guidance of the Holy Spirit both individually and as a church and be willing to recognize that the whole church may be wiser than any one individual or small group. Remember, too, that "the church" includes other ages as well as our own; when the whole weight of Christian tradition is against what our age believes is right, we need to move—as the church did in ordaining women—with very careful deliberation. Christians who "read, mark, learn, and inwardly digest" the words of Holy Scripture (Prayer Book, pp. 184 and 236) will understand that suffering and tension have been the lot of God's people throughout history (read Hebrews 11, for example), but that God's purpose is not thwarted by our failures. God asks us to be faithful, not to overwhelm all enemies. "Patience and comfort" (or "steadfastness and encouragement") are gifts promised to us through reliance on the Scriptures (Romans 15:4).

Finally, we need to understand that when the Prayer Book speaks of the Bible as the "rule and ultimate standard of faith," it does not mean that every word of the Bible contains the same authority. Martin Luther once spoke of the Bible as being like the manger at Bethlehem: containing the Christ Child but surrounded by much straw. That seems overly harsh, but most Christians would agree that they find the Twenty-third Psalm more valuable than the Fifty-eighth and the fifth chapter of St. Matthew of more help than the third chapter of Leviticus. And even straw serves a purpose: Mary would have been reluctant to place the newborn baby on bare planks, and even the "strawiest" parts of the Bible provide context and setting for the rest.

INTERPRETING THE BIBLE

The Bible is central to the life of the Episcopal Church; that can hardly be doubted. But if a visitor stood at the door of the church and asked each member of the congregation what the

Bible had said to them that morning, you would probably get as many replies as there were people present. One might mention having found help in dealing with an important business decision, another might have found guidance in coping with a personal crisis, still another might have been struck by the way a particular passage spoke to a current national issue, and another might say, "In all honesty, I can't remember what was read, but the choir anthem gave me the sense of peace that I really needed." It is very likely that the priest tried to explain the meaning of one of the passages in the sermon and that many of those present found it helpful. But, again, the help they found might range from a better understanding of the passage to guidance with a variety of particular personal and social problems.

Should the Bible always speak to everyone in the same way? Some Christians do try to make the Bible say the same thing to everyone and to suggest that everyone should understand it in the same way. But Episcopalians, as we have said, have traditionally found their unity in a common pattern of worship, and that has left them able to allow much more freedom in the reading and understanding of Holy Scripture. They expect that the readings on a given Sunday will speak to different people differently. They will also be aware that outside the Episcopal Church there is an even wider range of ways of understanding the Bible and that it may be helpful to realize that the Bible has been read and understood in very different ways in the past.

If you have a copy of the King James Version of the Bible, you might look at the chapter headings in the Song of Solomon. The text of this book seems to be about human love, and there are some rather erotic passages, but the chapter headings tell us it is about the mutual "Love of Christ and his Church" and "The church's love to Christ." Modern scholars differ as to whether the poem deals with the love of a man and a woman for each other or the love of God for the land of Israel. But an earlier day assumed that all Scripture dealt with our relationship with God and had to be interpreted that way.

Similarly, the New Testament twice cites an Old Testament verse (Deuteronomy 25:4) about muzzling an ox while it treads out the grain as evidence that a preacher should be paid (1 Corinthians 9:9 and 1 Timothy 5:18). Modern scholars would see it as evidence of a proper concern for the welfare of animals, but earlier generations assumed that there were deeper meanings to be found even in passages that seemed to have very little spiritual importance. A literal interpretation of the Bible requires us to accept the New Testament interpretation of the Old Testament; a more historical perspective allows us to understand the Old Testament passage in its own context and to accept the rather different approach of the New Testament writers without limiting ourselves to their particular interpretation. Earlier ages lacked the depth of historical understanding that we have gained; they judged everything in the terms of their own day, as Renaissance artists, for example, depicted biblical figures in Renaissance garb. Today, we understand that other ages have not all dressed alike and thought alike and we are less likely to try to squeeze their thoughts into the same mold.

Of course, we too are limited by our age and its expectations. Some Christians today would reject out of hand biblical passages that conflict with modern science, and some, on the other hand, would reject modern science where it seems to conflict with the Bible. Episcopalians generally have not gone to either of those extremes, but have found it better to try to read the words of the Bible with as full as possible an understanding of the situation of those who wrote and first heard them. To see and hear the Scriptures that way can then help us to interpret them for the needs and situation of our own times.

READING THE BIBLE

How then should Episcopalians read the Bible? Having heard it in the context of worship, how do we proceed to incorporate it more fully into our lives—or better, incorporate our lives more fully into it?

What we should not do is what almost every Bible reader has done at one time or another: open it at the first page and begin to read. We will do well enough for a few chapters, but quickly bog down in genealogies, unpronounceable names, and a vengeful bloodthirstiness that seems far removed from almost any vision of God we might have had before. Perhaps, then, these guidelines will be helpful:

1.   Don't begin at the beginning. The books of the Bible are not arranged in the order in which they were written or the order in which events took place. Some of the earliest material is found half-way through the Bible, in the Psalms. The Book of Daniel was written several centuries after the Book of Amos though it is placed before it in the Bible. The Gospel according to St. Matthew was probably written after the Gospel according to St. Mark. The Epistle to the Galatians was written before the Epistle to the Romans. Most Christians probably should read through the Bible end to end at some point, but a good place to begin is with the story of Jesus in one of the Gospels (Matthew, Mark, Luke, and John). After that, the Book of Genesis contains stories everyone should know, and the story of the Kingdom of David in 1 and 2 Samuel is not only great history but provides a picture of David, warts and all, that shows how God can be at work in a deeply flawed yet deeply responsive human life. The Book of

Acts gives us a picture of the early church and the travels of St. Paul. The Epistles to the Corinthians and Romans help us see how St. Paul gave early Christians guidance in church matters and daily living. Read one of these books through, then try another.

2. Look to the church for guidance. It has been said that the Bible is "the church's book." The Bible contains books that the church chose out of many others as being of particular value. The lectionaries at the back of the Prayer Book continue to provide the church's guidance as to which passages of the biblical books are of most value. The first five books of the Bible, with 186 chapters, are cited thirty-nine times in the Sunday lectionary, but so is the Book of Isaiah, with only 66 chapters.

3. Get help. In the early days of the church, Philip met a man who was reading the prophet Isaiah. When Philip asked him if he understood what he was reading, he replied, "How can I, unless someone guides me?" (Acts 8:26–39). The answer remains, "You probably can't." You don't absolutely need to know why the events of creation are told in one order in the first chapter of Genesis and the reverse order in the second chapter, but it will certainly help to have it explained. You don't have to know the difference between a Sadducee and a Pharisee, but it will be easier to understand the Gospels if you know something about these groups. A class at the church may help; a Bible study group can help a lot; a one-volume Bible commentary or an annotated Bible will be almost essential. Remember that almost all the Bible was written to and for communities and is still best read in a community. As we study the Bible with others, we gain a deeper and broader understanding from their insights—and they will gain from ours.

4.   Pray. The purpose of Bible study is the formation of a closer relationship with God; therefore, the Bible needs always to
be set in the context of prayer. God is more likely to speak to
you through the Bible if you ask God to do so.

5.   Set appropriate goals. Do not expect the Bible to advise
you as to which stocks to invest in or whom you should marry.
Do expect that you will make better decisions in these and
other areas if you have been reading the Bible prayerfully.

But do read the Bible. The Bible has been understood in
different ways in different times and is given varying interpretations and authority in our own day, but it has always guided, strengthened, and inspired those who have turned to it with
open minds and hearts. Long and learned commentaries have
been written about the Sermon on the Mount and exactly to
whom Jesus was referring when he said, "Blessed are the poor
in spirit." No doubt we can profit by a deeper study of those
words, but they speak to us whether we have done such study
or not. No particular scholarship or guidance is needed to find
value in passages like the Twenty-third Psalm, "The Lord is my
shepherd," or 1 Corinthians 13, "Love never ends." Some may
read the Book of Revelation and become possessed by the
thought that they can calculate the exact date of the end of the
world; others will find the passage that says, "Then I saw a new
heaven and a new earth; for the first heaven and the first earth
had passed away, and the sea was no more. And I saw the holy
city, the new Jerusalem, coming down out of heaven from God,
prepared as a bride adorned for her husband" (Revelation
21:1–2), and be inspired to work toward that vision by helping
in a soup kitchen or lobbying for improved programs for those
in need or by running for political office. Still others, bereaved

or lonely, will read, beginning with the next verse, "See, the home of God is among mortals. He will dwell with them as their God; they will be his peoples, and God himself will be with them; he will wipe every tear from their eyes. Death will be no more; mourning and crying and pain will be no more, for the first things have passed away," and they will hear it as the word they need and find new strength.

No wonder Episcopalians make such use of the Bible in public worship, in corporate study, and in private as well. Through it we come to know and be strengthened and guided by the God who calls us into the church to worship and sends us out to serve.

Questions for Further
Thought and Discussion:

1. The first section of this chapter lists three consequences of hearing the Bible within the worshiping community as opposed to reading it alone. If you could chose only one, which consequence would you say is most important to you? Why?

2. What are some of the things described in this chapter as what the Bible is not? How is the Bible described? Do you agree with all of the descriptions? How would you explain what the Bible is to someone who had never heard of it?

3. How much of the Bible would you estimate you've read? Of the guidelines for reading the Bible listed on pages 56–58, how many have you followed? Which one would you say has been the most helpful to you? Why? In what setting do you feel you have learned the most from the Bible?

The Church's Teaching

WHAT IS THEOLOGY?

No words are adequate to explain a great piece of music or work of art, but words can deepen our appreciation. What was it that moved us or inspired us? What did we see or hear in it that we would like others to understand? Such an explanation can be made only with words, so we attempt to put into words the meaning and significance of what we have seen or heard. But words have their limits, and any explanation we offer will fall short in one way or another. Some interpretations may be great works of art themselves, as for example Keats's "Ode on a Grecian Urn," but no words can ever fully explain to everyone's satisfaction what the art itself means—nor can the art itself fully reflect what it was that inspired the artist.

Theology is like that. It is an attempt to put into words what human beings have come to understand about God. It is never fully satisfactory, nor does it ever replace the need for individuals to come to know and respond to God directly themselves. Perhaps the question we need to bear in mind is, What is theology for? If it is intended to unite us around clear and definitive statements, we may well find ourselves divided instead. But if we look to worship to unite us and to theology to help us understand and express the God we encounter in worship, then theology comes into its own.

Christians come to know God through the witness of others, through the Bible, through prayer, and through music, nature, and art. They respond to that knowledge in many ways. But as a church, the primary experience of God for Episcopalians lies in our worship. Our theology, therefore, is based in very large part on that worship. We come in worship to a knowledge of God that surpasses words. We then attempt to find the best words we can to express and explain that knowledge. Furthermore, if we continue the comparison between music, art, and worship, we might also notice that while the liturgy is somewhat like a work of art, it is also different in that we do not simply admire it, we participate in it and even help to make it. This is the reason Christians sometimes speak of "doing theology." Theology is not simply statements that we accept or reject; it has a direct relationship to our way of living as Christians.

WORSHIP COMES FIRST

Episcopalians find their unity primarily in worship, an experience that lifts them beyond language and logic, but theology has to do with language and logic. It is not surprising, then, that Episcopalians do theology differently than do the members of many other churches. Episcopalians do care very much about language but they draw the language of theology primarily from the experience of worship and the language they use in speaking *to* God rather than *about* God. Thus the introduction of contemporary language into the Book of Common Prayer in 1979 led to long and angry disagreements among church members; how we talk to God matters. Sometimes the issue may have been as much or more about the sound of the

language as about its meaning, but beautiful language, like art
or music, expresses more than the simple meaning of the words;
the Elizabethan prose of the Prayer Book and the King James
Version of the Bible drew people who sometimes scarcely
understood what the words meant. The author, in fact, once
knew a Unitarian who came to the Eucharist with great regu-
larity every Sunday, but never received Communion. He dis-
agreed with the words, but loved the sound of them. Many
Episcopalians, likewise, have been accused of caring more
about the sound of the words than the meaning; yet the sound
of beautiful language has its own meaning and value, and the
new language in the Prayer Book simply expands our options.

Doing theology, then, is not an isolated activity for
Episcopalians. Those who still know Latin will quote the
ancient saying, "lex orandi, lex credendi," which means, freely
translated, "prayer shapes belief." Christians' prayer and worship are, of course, shaped by what they believe, but for
Episcopalians, what we believe is often learned through worship. Roman Catholics have traditionally turned to Thomas
Aquinas as a primary theological authority while Lutherans
have turned to Martin Luther and Presbyterians and members
of the reformed churches to John Calvin. The only compara-
ble figure in Anglicanism is Thomas Cranmer, who was not a
theologian but who produced the first Book of Common
Prayer. Episcopalians may come to a discussion of theology
later than other Christians, but might argue that they do it
better as a result of coming to it through worship.

The way Episcopalians do theology grows out of this primary Anglican concern for worship. Worship for example, is
inclusive, not exclusive, while theology, by its nature, excludes.
Theology is concerned with defining issues and boundaries,
with saying we believe this and not that. Worship, on the other
hand, like great music and art, can be appreciated on many

levels and in many ways. Art, music, and worship are difficult to define in words and it would be difficult to say that someone whose appreciation is different from ours is wrong. Worship, then, has the ability to unite, to draw us in and draw us together.

Episcopalians, as a result of this approach, have an inclusive understanding of the church. We baptize infants rather than limiting membership, as the Puritans did and as some other churches still do, to those who have had a conversion experience. We are not likely to quiz our fellow members about the depth or sincerity of their beliefs. Queen Elizabeth I once said, "I will not make windows into men's souls." Her concern was that the nation be united in worship but that no questions be asked as to why exactly people were there or what precisely they believed. If they were in the same building, using the same prayer book, that would provide a solid foundation on which Christians could build a mature faith.

Theology relies on language in its attempt to understand religious experience, and those who worship God know how difficult it is to put that experience into words. God is always beyond our definitions. That will be frustrating to those who want precise answers to all their questions but liberating to those who feel restricted and unsatisfied by some of the answers they have been given in the past. Definitive answers block off further inquiry, but limited answers stimulate the search for better answers and should lead to a lifelong process of growth and a thirst for a fuller knowledge of God that can only be fully satisfied hereafter in God's presence.

CREEDS AND THE EARLY CHURCH

If there are no final answers to be found in this life, where can we go to find preliminary answers that will at least lead us in the right direction? Anglicans have most often answered that question by speaking of "Scripture, tradition, and reason." The primary place of Scripture in Anglicanism has already been discussed. We must turn now to tradition and reason to understand more completely the Anglican approach to theology.

Beginning as we do with worship and a desire for unity, Anglicans have preferred to look for guidance to the undivided church, the church before it was divided by the Reformation, and especially to the first centuries of the church's life. Scripture, of course, is the primary written authority, but Scripture, as we have seen, is not always clear and does not answer all questions. Anglicans turn, therefore, to "tradition," the worship, teaching, and life of the church throughout the ages. No better summary of this tradition can be found than the Creeds agreed to by the church in its early days. Episcopalians recite the Nicene Creed at every Sunday celebration of the Eucharist, thus bringing faith and worship together in the closest possible way. The shorter, Apostles' Creed is recited at every baptism and at the Daily Offices of Morning and Evening Prayer. The bishops of the worldwide Anglican Communion have agreed that the Nicene Creed is "the sufficient statement of the Christian faith" (Prayer Book, p. 877). For a basic statement of what Episcopalians believe, then, we can begin with this Creed, accepted by all Christians and adopted in the fourth century by the first ecumenical councils.

A quick look at the Nicene Creed shows that it has three paragraphs and that they affirm belief in God the Father, in Jesus Christ, and in the Holy Spirit. God the Father is spoken of as Creator, Jesus is said to be "of one Being with the Father," and the Holy Spirit is said to be "worshiped and glorified" with the Father and the Son. The Creed has to do, first of all, with a Trinitarian God.

The second significant thing to notice about the Creed is that the second paragraph is the longest and that it has two themes: the unity of Jesus Christ with God the Father, and the human life that Jesus lived. The belief that the Son of God came into this world and lived a human life is summed up in the word "incarnation" (coming into flesh). God is best known in a human life.

But notice that the Creed does not explain the Trinity or the Incarnation; it simply asserts their truth. In the early centuries of the church's life, a number of possible explanations of Jesus' life were put forward. Perhaps, it was suggested, Jesus was simply a very good man or a divine being other than God; perhaps Father, Son, and Spirit are simply three aspects of God and God's essential nature is unity. The great ecumenical councils that met in the fourth and fifth centuries considered and rejected all these possibilities in favor of statements that rule out inadequate explanations without providing an explanation themselves. The Trinity and Incarnation remain mysteries; we can offer possible explanations and suggest ways of thinking about them that may be helpful, but the ultimate nature of God remains beyond human reason. It is appropriate, therefore, to put the Creed in the liturgy as part of our worship rather than insist on further explanations.

To say that the doctrines of the Trinity and of the Incarnation are mysteries is not, however, to say that they are unimportant. We may not be able to explain them, but they remain at the very center of our Christian life. *How* God could become incarnate cannot be explained; *that* God became incarnate is essential to our knowledge and understanding of God and to every aspect of our lives. If Jesus was simply a good man, our knowledge of God remains as limited as before; we are still not sure what God is like. But if God truly became a human being in the person of Jesus Christ, then we have seen in him, as much as we can ever see and know in this life, what God is like. Human beings can understand only in human

terms: in Jesus God has given us in human terms the fullest
possible statement of the nature of God and of God's care for
us. To say that God became incarnate in Jesus Christ is to say
that no fuller expression of God's love for us and will for us
can be given. How God could enter so fully into one human
life cannot be explained, but because God did so all human
life is changed.

In a similar way, the Trinity is the mystery on which our
lives depend. We cannot explain how God can be at one and
the same time an indivisible unity and yet have a threefold
nature. But the early Christians found themselves with no
other way to explain their experience. The most basic assertion
of the Judaism from which Christianity grew was that God is
One. Yet the first disciples knew in Jesus a human being of
whom they were compelled to say, "He is God." And then the
church experienced also an indwelling, guiding power that led
them to speak of a Holy Spirit and this Spirit, too, seemed to
be God. They knew there were not three gods, but they could
not dismiss their experience as simply three ways of knowing
God. It was also clear to them that this threefold nature of
God changed their prayer life and their daily living. Jesus had
come to teach and reveal and die and rise again and to be present with them in the gathered church and the breaking of the
bread. Jesus now lived to intercede for them at the throne of
God. That in itself changed their lives. But they also experienced the power of God at work within, moving them to pray,
guiding their prayer and their decisions, and enabling them to
accomplish more than they had ever imagined; this too was
God. So their lives were filled with God and united with God
and drawn toward God in a new and powerful way; to say anything less than that God was three-in-one would have been
inadequate to their experience. It made their prayer immediate and personal. The idea of Trinity, three persons in one

nature, did not completely explain their experience, but it ruled out other, inadequate explanations.

THE CATHOLIC FAITH

The Nicene Creed primarily affirms the Trinity and the Incarnation. Anglicans also have centered their attention on these two doctrines above all others. They are beliefs agreed to by all Christians (or, to put it the other way around: those who do not hold these beliefs are not Christians), and they remain beyond rational explanation; they remain mysteries, and the proper response to mystery is worship. Notice how the Creed as a theological statement functions to set boundaries or guidelines while, as a part of our worship, it functions to open our lives to the mystery of God. The Creed is not intended to end debate so much as to guide the ongoing search for explanations.

Of course, if Anglicans insist on statements of faith that all Christians hold, it is reasonable to ask what makes Anglicanism different, and the best answer is, "Nothing." A twentieth-century Anglican (J. V. L. Casserley) once entitled a book he had written *No Faith of My Own* as a way of pointing out that Anglicanism never intends to put forward new creeds or beliefs. We do not intend to believe anything that all Christians have not always believed. As Vincent of Lerins put it in the fifth century: the Catholic Church holds to "that which has been believed everywhere, always, and by all." The very word "catholic," meaning "universal," implies exactly that: catholic faith is universal faith, faith accepted by the whole church in all times and places.

It must be admitted that there are very few things that have been so widely accepted in the church as to meet Vincent of Lerins's criterion. Beyond the Trinity and Incarnation, we might have to turn to beliefs that have been accepted in most places, at most times, by most people. But even that somewhat lower standard can give us guidance. We need to check our ideas against those of others; if I find that an idea of mine is inconsistent with what most other Christians have generally believed, I could not proclaim it as the faith of the church and I ought to be very cautious about commending it to others. Anglicanism gives us great freedom in exploring and suggesting new ways of thinking but also insists that we are part of a church and cannot claim to be teaching the catholic faith if hardly anyone else sees it as we do.

One of the differences between Anglican and Roman versions of catholicism is that Anglicans have relied on the witness and teaching of the undivided church while Rome has been willing to adopt new doctrines and require belief in them. Thus in 1870, the First Vatican Council proclaimed the infallibility of the pope, and in 1950 the pope declared that the Virgin Mary had been bodily received into heaven and required church members to believe it. It would be difficult to maintain that these doctrines meet Vincent of Lerins's standard of catholic faith since there have obviously been many Christians of all times and places who did not accept these ideas. When Anglicans appeal to tradition as a guide, they are speaking first of all about the early and undivided church and then about the continuing witness of Christians in every age. The Roman Church, on the other hand, includes papal teaching in its understanding of tradition.

In emphasizing the faith of the whole church, the Anglican approach is different not only from the Roman approach centered on the authority of one individual but also from the strong tendency toward individualism that has often been noticed in studies of American society. Robert Bellah, for example, in a book called *Habits of the Heart* cited a woman named Sheila, who described her faith as "Sheilaism." She said, "I believe in God. I'm not a religious fanatic. I can't

remember the last time I went to church. My faith has carried
me a long way. It's Sheilaism. Just my own little voice."[1]
Whatever else that may be, it is not the catholic faith! Worship
begins with a corporate expression of faith and that leads in
turn to a theology that is corporate, expressing the faith of the
church, not the individual.

REASON

Anglicans have, as we said earlier, appealed to Scripture, tradition, and reason as the basis on which to build an understanding of God. No matter how much some Christians may
question reliance on human reason, they cannot avoid using
their minds to do so. Neither Scripture nor tradition provides
clear and certain answers to all questions; at some point, there
is no way to decide among possible interpretations except
through the use of the human mind. This is not a blank check
for Sheilaism, however; part of what makes a decision reasonable is the knowledge that many others have come to the same
or similar conclusions. It would be quite unreasonable to take
an unidentified pill in the hope that it would do me good; I
would want to find out what others could tell me about it first.
And even if a doctor I had known and trusted for many years
were to recommend that I undergo major surgery, I would
probably think it was reasonable to get a second opinion and
perhaps other opinions as well. Reason involves study and
investigation and consultation, as well as careful, critical thinking and reflection, not a sudden feeling or individual impulse.
It does, however, include the intuitive use of the mind; "reason," as Anglicans use the term, includes both "right brain"
and "left brain" activity. Anglicans have traditionally shown a
great respect for reason and, indeed, have copied into the symbol of the Anglican Communion known as the "Compasrose"
the words of St. John's Gospel, "The truth will make you free"

(8:32). Quoting Scripture or listening to the pope is all very well, but I have an obligation also to use my mind as far as I can. Reason is a gift of God; it cannot be ignored or silenced. Indeed, the use of human reason is a way of participating in the divine reason, the mind of God who creates all things in wisdom.

Toward the end of the sixteenth century, when the Church of England was attempting to understand its new life in separation from Rome and in distinction from the great reform movements on the continent of Europe, a priest named Richard Hooker wrote a book called *The Laws of Ecclesiastical Polity*, which has continued to influence Anglican thought. In it, Hooker says that Christians should look for guidance not from the pope or simply from the Bible, but from Scripture, tradition, and reason. We begin with Scripture, learn what the church has traditionally taught, and use our minds to understand. These three work together to give Anglicans a balanced approach to understanding the faith of the church. Try sometime to make a stool stand on one leg or two, or notice how a four-legged chair or table wobbles when put down on an uneven floor—but a three-legged stool will always be stable.

Another and better known leader in the generation after Hooker was John Donne, a poet and preacher, who was first to speak of the Anglican path as a "middle way" or *via media*. The Anglican way, as he saw it, was to steer a course between the extremes of no reform and radical reform, between Rome on the one hand and the new Protestant churches on the other. Sometimes that has been misunderstood to mean compromise or fence-sitting, but neither of those alternatives is intended. Rather the intention has been to achieve a comprehensiveness or breadth of approach that could draw wisdom from every side and include the insights of others. We have already mentioned Bishop Hobart of New York and his motto of "evangelical faith and apostolic order," which is one way to express the comprehensiveness that Anglicanism seeks to achieve. Anglican theology prefers to avoid either/or choices, thinking that there is often more wisdom in both/and.

A both/and approach, of course, runs the risk of creating tension between those who prefer one side or the other—as most of us often do. The classic illustration of this is the tension within Anglicanism that has been reflected in terms such as "high church" and "low church" or "evangelical" and "catholic." These labels reflect, rather inadequately, the difference between those whose faith is centered first on the church with its liturgy and sacraments (high church) and those whose faith centers primarily on the Bible and the preaching of the Word (low church). At its best, the Episcopal Church is not one or the other, but both. The catholic faith must be proclaimed to those outside, and the proclamation of the word should draw people to Christ in the church. The church is enriched by the presence within its life of these complementary emphases.

THE TENSIONS OF COMPREHENSIVENESS

There will, of course, always be some who, for reasons of education or temperament or experience, are so strongly attracted to one aspect of the church's life that they neglect the other. The emotional impact of the two emphases, for example, is often quite different. The evangelical approach may be more personal and subjective and appeal to those whose life experiences have given them a deep sense of sin and of a need to be set free from that burden. John Newton's great hymn speaks of the "amazing grace... that saved a wretch like me; I once was lost, but now am found..." Someone whose life has been damaged by alcohol or drugs and who at last is able to break their grip on his or her life may feel that sense of freedom and thankfulness very deeply. Someone, on the other hand, who was baptized as an infant, who grew up in the church, and who has known Christ's presence in the sacraments, will respond less strongly to Newton's hymn than to a hymn such as "The Church's One Foundation." One experience may be seen as more subjective, the other as more objective; one rejoices that "I have been saved," the other that "God comes to us;" one centers more on the individual's subjective experience, the other on the objective reality of God's presence in church and sacraments. Both are true, but it is difficult for one individual to keep them in balance. A comprehensive church, however, needs both perspectives.

Though emphases have varied through the centuries, Anglican theology has probably tended more toward the objective and catholic perspective. Given the church's history, this may be understandable. If a primary concern has been unity within the church and the avoidance of division, emotions may be seen as dangerous. But the result has sometimes been division nonetheless. In the eighteenth century, John Wesley's Methodist movement proved too much for a church that was fearful of such enthusiasm and the result was the tragic division between the Methodists and the Church of England and the Episcopal Church.

The same tension can be seen in the different emphases that Anglican theologians bring to their explanations of the Christian faith. A simple summary of the Christian faith might say that God created a good world but human beings misused their freedom and rebelled against God; therefore, God came into this world and died for us to set us free from sin and open the way to eternal life. But individual experience has often led Christians to center their attention either on creation and Incarnation or on sin and redemption. Anglican theology at its best has affirmed both, but Anglican theology has often been drawn to one side or the other and, most often, to the side of creation and Incarnation. There is much to be gained from theologians whose thought has been centered on this aspect of Christian faith: a deep understanding of creation would lead to a concern for the environment, and a deep understanding of the Incarnation would lead to a concern for all the problems that face human society. Episcopalians have often been committed to social action, feeling responsible to help renew the earth and human society. But that approach, lacking a sense of human sin and the need for redemption, can lead to a political agenda that fails to deal with the individual's need for a personal relationship with God in Christ. Conversely, a focus on individual redemption can overlook the need to reform society and its institutions. Both/and is a difficult path to follow and few individuals or even parish churches will succeed. The larger church, however, usually has individuals and congregations and larger organizations acting out of insights and convictions that, together, make up the wholeness that is needed. Catholics are not allowed to forget the need for evangelism, and evangelicals are reminded that the corporate life of the church is needed also.

OTHER ISSUES

If Episcopalians set out to believe only those things that all Christians believe, why are not all American Christians Episcopalians? Perhaps they should be (!), but, in fact, not all Christians agree that the Creed is a "sufficient statement" of the Christian faith. They may not disagree with the Creed, but they want agreement on other matters as well. To be honest, Episcopalians also, when involved in discussions about Christian unity, will often insist on agreement in other areas. The Nicene Creed resolved the issues troubling the early church, but there were other issues that had not yet been fully examined or on which agreement was assumed in that time. When these issues emerged for discussion at the time of the Reformation, it was discovered that disagreement on these subjects ran so deep that Christians were unable to remain in unity. Among these issues were the nature of the church, the ministry, and the sacraments. The Nicene Creed affirms faith in "one, holy, catholic, and apostolic church" and a "baptism for the forgiveness of sins," but that is not much help when specific questions are raised.

Consider, for example, the church and the ministry. Is the oneness and catholicity of the church dependent on the authority of the pope or the authority of the Bible? Anglicans have tended to claim that unity and catholicity depend on the claim to be "apostolic" and that an apostolic church must have bishops as successors of the apostles to provide visible continuity with the apostolic church. This does seem to have been the belief and practice of the early church, but is it essential today? Some Episcopalians have gone so far as to divide all Christians into two camps: the catholic church, which has bishops (Roman Catholics, Anglicans, the Eastern Orthodox, and a few others), and the Protestant churches, which, lacking bishops, lack the catholic faith. There have even been times when small groups of Episcopalians have followed a bishop off into the wilderness, comfortable in the feeling that they had the vital symbol of unity even though they were now divided from all other Christians. But what use is a symbol of unity that leaves the church in splinters? More recently, a consensus seems to be growing that while bishops are a valuable symbol of the church's unity through the ages and a vital element in any reunited Christian church, it is not necessary to insist on a particular definition of the meaning of the bishop's role. In Europe and the United States, a deeper relationship with Lutherans has been developed on this basis, and it may be that a path toward greater unity with other Christians is opening up as well. Unity does not require uniformity. Careful and narrow definitions, as Anglicans have long known, are seldom helpful in promoting unity.

DOING THEOLOGY TODAY

The theologians of the early church were intent on creating statements of faith that would help resolve the divisions in the church and that would make sense to the world around them. When they used the words we find in the Creeds, words like "person" and "nature," they were using Greek words that philosophers of the ancient world knew and understood but that may not mean exactly the same thing in modern English. Modern theologians struggle to find better ways to express these ideas to our society but must always be guided by the words that Christians have recited through the centuries and the meaning behind those words. For many Christians, however, the real issues of the moment lie in a different area.

For most of the history of the human race, for example, gender defined roles. In many societies, men went out hunting or fighting; women stayed home and raised children. Since men played the dominant role in society, they naturally used masculine language to speak of God. By the end of the twentieth century, however, the western world had created a society in which men and women were far more free to define their roles without reference to gender. Women, too, could be chief executives or priests or bishops, and the traditional language about God began to seem too narrow and limited.

When Christians thought about this, they realized that the Bible, although dominated by masculine imagery, did include imagery about God that was feminine: the Bible spoke of God giving birth to God's people in travail (Deuteronomy 32:18); Jesus spoke of wanting to gather people together as a hen gathers chickens under her wings (Matthew 23:37). As theologians explored these matters, it became obvious that there was a need not simply for inclusive imagery in gender terms, but in other terms as well. We have centered attention on the image of God as king and shepherd, but God is also described in the

Bible as a rock and a fire and a "still, small voice." For Anglicans, the question must be whether our worship has done justice to these images and whether it might be enriched by a fuller use of the language suggested by the Bible itself.

Changes in theological language are always somewhat threatening and, for Episcopalians, these changes can be especially upsetting, because they deal with our worship and, therefore, our immediate relationship with God. But language is not God; it simply points toward God, and it does that more or less adequately depending on its ability to engage people of a particular time and place. Christians of the very rational eighteenth century thought of God as a clockmaker, and that worked well as long as the universe could be imagined to resemble a clock or piece of machinery. Darwin and Einstein, however, have produced a very different picture of the universe God has made, a universe of mysterious relationships and constant change. The God who created and indwells this universe breaks through whatever language we use, but we will limit our understanding of God unnecessarily if we remain tied down by the language of past ages.

Episcopalians, it could be argued, are better able to deal with such issues than most other Christians. They have never been tied to a particular theological system. They know that words can only point toward God, but cannot define or capture God. They have understood that it is better to expand their understanding of God with terms like both/and rather than restrict it by requiring a choice of either/or. Most of all, they value the freedom they have to explore new and better ways of expressing the truth that is found in Christ. Such freedom is not always easy to live with, but Episcopalians believe that the challenge to grow into new enrichment is a reward that is worth the price.

QUESTIONS FOR FURTHER
THOUGHT AND DISCUSSION:

1. If the Creed is a "sufficient statement of the Christian faith," what issues have caused Episcopalians and other Christians to remain divided? Is it necessary to resolve any or all of those issues in order for a true reunion to be possible?

2. What is the *via media*? Can you give an example of a current issue in which the *via media* has proven to be a means of maintaining unity in the church?

3. What do the terms "evangelical" and "catholic" mean to you? How is it that a "both/and" approach to these two viewpoints can work within the Episcopal Church?

---

1. Robert Bellah, ed., *Habits of the Heart: Individualism in American Life* (Berkeley and Los Angeles: University of California Press, 1985), p. 221.

Spirituality

THE SOURCES

No one knows when Christianity first came to the British Isles, but there is a legend that Joseph of Arimathea, who gave the tomb for Jesus' burial, came to Britain after the Resurrection, bringing the cup that was used at the Last Supper, and that he built a church at Glastonbury, in southwestern England. If so, there may have been a church in England before there was one in Rome. Whether or not that is true, it is clear that Christianity came to England at a very early date since three British bishops attended a synod in France in A.D. 314 and other British bishops attended the Council of Nicaea in A.D. 325. But pagan Germanic tribes called Angles and Saxons invaded Britain in the sixth century and pushed the British church into Wales and Ireland. Before long, however, this early British or Celtic church pushed back with amazing energy, sending missionaries into Scotland and the north of England, then into the Low Countries and Germany, and finally as far east as the Ukraine and as far south as Italy. Nonetheless, it was the Roman Church, moving north, which began the conversion of the Anglo-Saxons in the year A.D. 597, when Pope Gregory sent a man called Augustine, who began his work by founding a church in southeastern England at Canterbury. That Roman mission from the south finally met the Celtic Church from the north, and at a synod in Whitby in the year A.D. 664 that was called to resolve the differences between them, the Celtic Church agreed to adopt the Roman pattern of Christianity.

Nonetheless, the Celtic approach left its mark on the church in England. The Celtic Church was much more loosely organized than the Roman Church; it had monastic communities as centers of teaching and mission rather than territorial dioceses centered on a bishop. In the Celtic system, the abbot ruled the monastery and the surrounding area as father of a family, while the Roman bishop directed the administration of the diocese as an overseer. The Celtic Church also made few distinctions between roles for men and roles for women; women were ordained to the priesthood and consecrated as bishops in Ireland as early as the seventh century. Celtic Christianity also was closer to nature and thought more intuitively about the faith. It was, as we have learned to say, more "right brained" in its approach. The great hymn known as "St. Patrick's Breastplate" and attributed to St. Patrick reflects that way of thinking. It feels the presence of God in nature, in "the flashing of the lightning free, the whirling wind's tempestuous shocks, the stable earth, the deep salt sea around the old, eternal rocks."[1] And it feels Christ's presence in human life: "Christ within me... Christ beside me... Christ in mouth of friend and stranger." The familiar children's hymn that begins, "All things bright and beautiful, all creatures great and small,"[2] shows that this type of spirituality was still influential in nineteenth-century England. When we sing these hymns today, we feel again the impact of Celtic Christianity. In recent years there has been a more deliberate effort to recover this

part of Anglicanism's spiritual heritage, so much in tune with
our own concerns for the environment and our renewed
appreciation of the intuitive element in human nature.

Although the Roman form of Christianity became the
dominant influence in Britain as in all of western Europe,
Anglican Christianity has continued to have a distinctive qual-
ity because of its Celtic heritage. Anglican Christianity has
been less apt to seek legal and administrative solutions to problems; it has stressed the pastoral nature of Christian ministry;
it is freer in its relationship to authority; and it has been more
willing to adopt intuitive modes of thought.

It is also significant that St. Augustine, who brought the
Roman form of Christianity to England, was a Benedictine
monk and came with a company of monks of that order. For
almost a thousand years, the Benedictine Order was predomi-
nant in England, and it has continued to shape the Anglican
way of life. Benedictines established small communities like a
family, centered on a balanced life of work and prayer. As in
Celtic Christianity, the Benedictine abbot functioned as a
father rather than as an administrator and community problems were resolved through consultation rather than a narrow
adherence to laws. The emphasis was on reason and modera-
tion. Even though the bishops were established in cities and
larger towns and administered their dioceses in the Roman
manner, the abbeys, established always in remote country
areas, exerted a very strong influence in what was still a land of
farmers and shepherds. England was known in the Middle
Ages as "the land of the Benedictines."

The mystical element in religion is also an important aspect
of the Anglican heritage. During some periods of history, mys-
ticism has been looked at with great suspicion: it isn't logical and
rational, it relies instead on intuition and feelings. But there have
always been some Christians whose lives were strongly affected

by this intuitive sense of God's presence. Fourteenth-century England, in particular, produced a number of men and women whose direct experience of God has continued to inspire and influence others. Among these were Julian of Norwich, Margery Kempe, Richard Rolle, Walter Hilton, and the unknown mystic who wrote a book called *The Cloud of Unknowing*. Julian was an anchorite, living in a small cell attached to a parish church. Margery Kempe was an illiterate housewife who traveled widely. Richard Rolle was a solitary hermit. Julian saw vivid images of Christ's suffering, Margery Kempe was overtaken by fits of weeping for the world's sins, and the author of *The Cloud* advised the avoidance of all imagery in mental prayer. It is hard to imagine a wider variety of types of spiritual life, but each has its particular value, and all of them provide rich resources for us to draw on today.

Still another significant influence on Anglicanism has come from Greece and Russia and the Orthodox churches of eastern Europe. The Reformation itself grew in part out of the rediscovery of the ancient Greek and Roman world. The Renaissance, with its rebirth of learning and its effort to rediscover the foundations of western civilization, enabled Christians to gain a new perspective on the medieval church and to see that there were other ways of living out the Christian faith. We have already spoken of the way the English reformers turned to the early centuries of the church's life for inspiration and guidance. The theologians of the early church were largely Greek, so it was logical for the Church of England, now separated from Rome, to look to the eastern church, separated from Rome five centuries earlier, and to find patterns there for its own life. The Orthodox Church, like the Celtic Church, was not a church controlled by laws and administrators; it had a more mystical sense of religion and centered its life in the liturgy. English theologians, looking east, found there a church with which they felt they had much in common.

The Prayer Book of the American Episcopal Church reveals the influence of eastern Christianity in several specific places. Most significant, perhaps, is the fact that there is an invocation of the Holy Spirit in the eucharistic prayer of consecration. The Roman Church in the Middle Ages had focused its attention on the so-called Words of Institution, the words Jesus spoke at the Last Supper, and came to believe that those words were the critical element in the transformation of the bread and wine into the body and blood of Christ. The Eastern Church, on the other hand, had centered its attention on an invocation of the Holy Spirit over the gifts. Archbishop Laud, in the seventeenth century, gave the Scottish Church a Prayer Book that included this invocation. The Scottish Church, in turn, commended this pattern to Bishop Seabury, who was able to include it in the first American Prayer Book. Thus the Episcopal Church has been linked from the beginning with the Orthodox Church at the very center of the Eucharist. The 1979 Prayer Book added still further forms of prayer drawn from eastern liturgies, ranging from the opening acclamation in Easter season to Eucharistic Prayer D (pp. 372–75) and the opening words of the Commendation at a Burial (pp. 482–83 and 499). The sacred pictures called icons, which are always found in Orthodox churches, have also become very popular in the Episcopal Church in recent years.

A very strong influence on Anglicanism, of course, was the Reformation, the great explosion that divided and renewed the western church in the middle of the sixteenth century. Although the English Church was insulated to some degree from the bitter divisions among Lutherans, Calvinists, and Rome by the English Channel and by the resistance of Henry VIII to reformed theology, there were many in England who found hope and inspiration in the work of Luther and Calvin and worked hard to reshape the English Church in accordance with their teachings. Though the most radical Puritans eventually lost hope for the full reformation they sought and left to colonize New England, more moderate reformers remained active in the church and established a strong evangelical witness that has inspired successive waves of renewal in later centuries.

Not to be overlooked in any discussion of spirituality in the Episcopal Church is the influence of the New World. From the very beginning in New England and almost from the beginning elsewhere, Anglicanism has been a very small part of an enormously complex religious picture that includes the major European churches (Roman, Lutheran, and Reformed), denominations like Baptists and Methodists that first flourished on the frontier, newer independent churches identified simply as evangelical and Pentecostal, and a variety of American-born denominations on or beyond the fringes of traditional Christianity, like the Seventh-Day Adventists, Christian Scientists, Mormons, and Jehovah's Witnesses. Judaism, too, has been a presence in the American colonies from an early time and that fact has served to make American Christians especially aware of their Jewish heritage. In the latter part of the twentieth century, as American society began to feel the impact of Asian and Arab immigrants, the church began to respond as well to some of the insights of eastern religion and to explore the possibility of dialogue with representatives of the Muslim faith. The need to communicate its unique witness in so varied a marketplace and without the inherited wealth of the Church of England has produced a church more concerned for outreach, evangelism, and stewardship. It has produced a church increasingly willing to borrow good ideas from the church down the block—and from

more distant groups as well. The American setting has also
helped make the Episcopal Church more democratic in structure and more open to change than any other church governed
by bishops.

In short, the spirituality of the Episcopal Church has been
shaped by no single confession of faith or theological system
but by a rich variety of sources, each adding unique values and
insights on which all may draw.

THE PATTERN

As a result of this blend of influences, the Episcopal Church
has centered its attention more often on the creation and
Incarnation than on sin and redemption. It has preferred to
praise God rather than dwell on humanity's failures. But sin is
a central fact of human life, twisting and destroying life at
every level, from the most personal and individual to the
national and international. Human beings have need of a
Savior and the good news of the gospel ("evangel," based on
the Greek word for gospel, means good news) is that God has
provided such a Savior. A relationship with Jesus Christ
changes lives. The evangelical insistence on the reality of the
sin that alienates human beings from their Creator, making
them dependent on God's redeeming grace, provides essential
balance to a creation-Incarnation focus that can begin to substitute reason for faith. Yet a narrow focus on sin and salvation
can become too subjective and individual, causing us to lose
sight of the need for the church to foster spiritual growth for
those being drawn to salvation. Either focus can easily cause
the loss of a balanced presentation of Christian teaching.
Anglicanism, at its best, has realized that no one system can
contain the whole of God's truth and has not relied on the
teaching of any single, dominating theologian. Instead,
Anglicans have recognized that almost every important question

has a range of possible answers. So they have taken a broad and inclusive approach and been willing to draw on insights from a variety of sources and to accept a both/and approach rather than confront people with an either/or decision.

In analyzing sin, Anglicans ordinarily avoid a simplistic identification of sin with certain specific behavior patterns or substances. Creation is good, however prone we are to abuse it. From the time of the Puritans, there have been American sects that have attempted to avoid sin by avoiding contact with societies that seemed to be beyond redemption and by condemning a variety of material things and behavior patterns— from candles, stained glass, and vestments to dancing, card playing, and alcohol. The attempt to identify sin with some outward enemy can also lead to such phenomena as racism, homophobia, obsessive anti-communism, a fear of the United Nations and international involvement, and a negative approach to the world in general. The Anglican approach, on the other hand, is positive and understands that sin lies in the misuse of good things rather than in the things themselves. The purpose of the spiritual life is to seek God's glory rather than simply to avoid sin. Nature has an inherent goodness that can be perfected by grace.

In the same way, an emphasis on the Incarnation leads to the understanding that the Christian faith is centered on God's presence in the world in human flesh. Christianity therefore is concerned for the whole of life, not for the soul alone apart from the body or for "spiritual things" as distinct from material things.

THE PRACTICE

How is all this expressed in real life? What specific guidance is provided for individuals seeking to grow in faithfulness? Many people today adopt a diet and have a regular program of physical exercise, and many are also beginning to discover the value of spiritual exercise as well. Our knowledge of the things that contribute to physical health, however, is a rather young science, but the church has centuries of experience to draw on in spiritual exercise. Many of the latest spiritual fads are, in fact, simply modern versions of ancient wisdom. The Book of Common Prayer—a good place to begin—provides a surprisingly detailed description of a well-ordered Christian life. The Prayer Book does not, however, set that description out on page one so that rules seem to be primary, nor does it threaten punishment here or hereafter for failures of any kind. It assumes that church members are, or seek to be, mature, competent human beings capable of taking responsibility for their own growth and are motivated by love, not fear.

The pattern begins, of course, with the Eucharist. The opening sentence on the first page after the table of contents and preface tells us that the Holy Eucharist is "the principal act of Christian worship on the Lord's Day"(p. 13). That reminds us that spirituality, in the Anglican tradition, begins with life shared in the church. Spirituality is not a matter of individual Christians coming together for occasional worship, but of a church whose members find their center in common worship and go out to serve according to the gifts and opportunities they are given in daily life.

The same first sentence goes on to tell us something of enormous significance: that Daily Morning and Evening Prayer are the other "regular services appointed for public worship in this Church." This is important for two reasons. First, the pattern provided for worship assumes a "daily" offering; Christian life is not thought of as something involving only one day a week. Second, one pattern of prayer is provided for all; there is no suggestion that daily prayer is something for clergy only. The idea that all members of the church should participate in a daily office goes back to Archbishop Cranmer. Although only a small minority of church members may actually live by this standard, it remains a significant ideal. By the Middle Ages, the Eucharist had become a "priest's mass" at which lay people were only spectators, and the daily offices were for those under monastic rule. So sharp was this separation and so peripheral was the role of the laity that those who were ordained were spoken of as "going into the church" and the term "spirituality" became a title for the clergy as a group—not at all what we mean when we use the word today. The reformed churches often reacted to this unfortunate separation by eliminating all distinction between clergy and lay people and reducing daily prayer to private prayer and Bible reading. The Anglican tradition, on the other hand, requires the involvement of priests and lay people in every Eucharist and sets out a daily pattern of prayer for all. The statement on page 13 of the Prayer Book says very clearly that lay people are to take a significant role in the liturgy.

Perhaps to encourage wider use of a pattern of daily prayer, the 1979 Prayer Book adds to the two traditional offices four much shorter forms of prayer for morning, midday, early evening, and the close of day (pp. 136–40). These provide only brief readings from the Bible and move away from Cranmer's vision of regular, systematic reading of the whole Bible. Cranmer, though, was creating a pattern for a society still largely illiterate and in which books were still expensive luxuries; most people in the sixteenth century would be exposed to the Bible only by hearing it read. Today, when most people own Bibles and many take part in Bible study groups, it is surely possible for people to make the Bible an important part of their lives apart from the Daily Office. Thus the new shortened forms of prayer may combine with private Bible reading and a Bible study group to provide as solid a foundation as the one Cranmer had hoped people would derive from the Daily Office.

The first stated goal of the first English Prayer Book was that the Bible be read in a systematic way. The last sixty-five pages of the 1979 Prayer Book (pp. 936–1001) still provide a program for daily reading of the Bible. Reading the Bible also implies study, and study requires resources. These would include books and articles as well as the opportunity to read and discuss the Bible with other church members. Knowledge of the circumstances in which the various books of the Bible were written can enable us to understand better how they can help and guide us today. But study is not simply to learn facts, however interesting, or to discover simple answers to our questions; the objective always is to enter into a relationship with the Scriptures, allowing them to surprise and challenge and question us. And this, in turn, is valuable only as it leads us into a deeper relationship with God through Jesus Christ.

The opening statement of the Prayer Book ("Concerning the Service of the Church") also has a good deal to say about music in worship (p. 14). Spirituality is shaped by music in important ways. Music helps to draw a congregation together and to provide a feeling of unity. It also shapes our faith through exposure to the beliefs of those who wrote the words and composed the music. These come from all the major Christian traditions and almost every century. We sing the faith of John Wesley, Martin Luther, Thomas Aquinas, Francis of Assisi, and Gregory the Great; we sing the faith of the Greek Church, the Russian Church, and the African-American Church—not to mention those of the Bible itself.

The diversity of Prayer Book sources is reflected in an entirely different way in the Calendar of Holy Days that takes almost twenty pages of the Prayer Book (pp. 15–33). Here we are asked to remember annually men and women of every age and place. Few of them are "household names," but many of them, as we come to know who they are, can inspire and strengthen us by their witness. Again and again, we are reminded that Prayer Book spirituality is not a spirituality of lonely souls and isolated seekers but a spirituality of the "communion of saints."

These early pages of the Prayer Book also make reference to fasting and list the times and seasons when abstinence and fasting are appropriate (p. 17). Most Fridays, for example, are listed as days of abstinence, days to remember Jesus' death, just as Sundays are feast days, celebrating the Resurrection. What the Prayer Book does not do, however, is to provide specific details as to what fasting and abstinence might mean. It does not say that Episcopalians are required to eat fish on Friday or abstain from meat; instead it speaks more broadly of "special acts of discipline and self-denial." The church understands that individual needs and abilities vary widely and that hamburger may be more penitential than salmon or rainbow trout. It is up to the individual to decide what acts of self-denial may be most helpful—though individual Christians should look always for guidance in such decisions through prayer and study and from others with greater experience. We live in an age when discipline and self-denial are a familiar part of life, though we may refer only to "exercise and diet." Contemporary exercise and diet, however, are self-centered and focused on the physical, while the discipline and self-denial recommended by the church are God-centered and focused on the spiritual. It is often said that "it's better to take things on than to give things up," but most people today live such full lives, they would be unable to take on anything more without giving something up first. Self-denial is a valuable way of remembering that there are few things we truly need except God. It is also an appropriate way to live in a world with finite resources in which too many are hungry and lack the riches others too easily take for granted. And it is biblical: Jesus said, "*Whenever* you fast…" not "if" (Matthew 6:16).

Fasting is only one example of the ways in which the Prayer Book commends biblical practices for spiritual growth. Jesus also said, "Whenever you give alms…" and "When you pray…" (Matthew 6:2–15). Likewise the Prayer Book tells us that it is "the duty of all Christians… to work, pray, and give for the spread of the kingdom of God" (p. 856). A disciplined use of all our resources begins with systematic giving of our selves, time, talent, and treasure to the work of the church. Jesus was very realistic in saying "where your treasure is, there your heart will be also" (Matthew 6:21). We can hardly be serious about spiritual growth if we keep our spiritual commitment in one compartment and our material resources in another. Anglicanism is, as we have said, an "incarnational" faith; it takes seriously the created order and expects that we will bring the whole of our lives into relationship with our faith. The Episcopal Church has acted through its General Convention to declare that stewardship is the most important work of Christians and to establish the tithe as the normal standard of Christian giving.

There can hardly be anything more important in spiritual growth than the time we spend in prayer both with others and by ourselves. The Prayer Book tells us that prayer is "responding to God, by thought and by deeds, with or without words" (p. 856). The Eucharist and Daily Offices provide two of the three strands of prayer for church members. Here we learn to pray with words drawn from twenty centuries of Christian life and experience. Private prayer, the third strand of prayer, is enriched by this background since the words and patterns of the Prayer Book come inevitably to our lips and shape our thoughts, guiding us into a deeper expression than we would be likely to produce from our own resources. But this is only a beginning; Christians will naturally go on from this foundation to become comfortable using their own words and, as the Prayer Book says, to pray "without words" as well. Our response to God in "deeds" will be discussed in the final chapter of this book.

The Prayer Book reminds also us that there are many kinds of prayer: adoration, praise, thanksgiving, penitence, oblation, intercession, and petition. Prayer is not simply turning to God for help in times of trouble or with a list of needs; it is not confined to asking for help for people who are sick or dying. Just as our conversation with those close to us is not limited to requests, so, too, conversation with God will normally include expressions of gratitude, entreaties for pardon, and the offering of ourselves. The purpose of prayer is not primarily to acquire something but to fulfill our baptismal identity; it has been described by Frank Griswold, the Presiding Bishop of the Episcopal Church, as "an openness to love at every level of our being."

The largest part of our time with those close to us is, of course, spent in silence. We may have nothing particular to say, but we are glad to be with those we care about, nonetheless. So, too, in our relationship with God, we should become comfortable in "lifting up the heart and mind to God, asking nothing but to enjoy God's presence" (p. 857). In recent years, the practice of "centering prayer," a pattern that can be traced back at least to the fourteenth-century teacher who wrote *The Cloud of Unknowing*, has helped many Christians learn the value of simply being present to God. But today as then, there will be some Christians who prefer to pray by making use of mental images, picturing, as Julian of Norwich did, the suffering of Christ on the cross or finding, as she did, natural images, like a hazelnut, that open our minds to the costliness of God's love and the wonder of God's care for us.

An interesting example of the way the church draws on the wisdom of various spiritual traditions is the increasing use of "mantras." Though the term comes from eastern religions such as Zen Buddhism that use a repeated word or phrase to concentrate the thoughts, the "Jesus prayer," from the Orthodox tradition, uses the same technique for a similar purpose. There are several slightly different versions of this prayer, but its essence is the repetition of the words, "Lord Jesus Christ, have mercy on me." The two phrases are synchronized with the natural process of breathing; the person praying breathes in while saying the first phrase and breathes out with the second phrase. Ideally, the prayer becomes as natural and instinctive as breathing itself, moving in and out of one's consciousness depending on the other demands of daily life. This kind of prayer is very much in keeping with the purpose of the Prayer Book pattern, which is not simply to say prayers and read the Bible, but to develop "habitual recollection," a constant sense of God's presence in the whole of life.

Although the experience of Prayer Book worship and the guidance provided in the questions and answers of the Catechism (pp. 856–57) are a very good place to begin, a growing number of church members are finding value in more personal counsel. Many also find support in the life of prayer through meeting regularly with a parish prayer group. Most parishes have at least one such group, and although many of these concentrate on intercessory prayer, others take a broader approach to prayer, and some specialize in forms of silent prayer such as centering prayer. Some prayer groups also give themselves to the biblical gift of praying in "tongues" and find that the experience of that type of prayer is powerfully enriching. Meetings for "prayer and praise" have become an important part of the spiritual life of many parishes.

Spiritual guidance comes also, of course, from sermons and reading as well as from informal conversation with priests or other fellow Christians. But rapidly growing numbers of individuals in recent years have come to value a "soul friend" or spiritual director. This relationship can be as simple as a regular meeting with another Christian to share experience in prayer and to learn from each other, and as formal as a regular meeting with a skilled, or a trained and "professional," spiritual director who can assess the individual's abilities and progress and provide the guidance needed to lead the individual into a deeper and richer relationship with God.

One further resource of great value is the wide variety of religious orders and retreat centers in the Episcopal Church. The religious orders, some for men and some for women, follow rules of life, often based on the ancient Benedictine pattern. Some of the orders have active ministries in schools and hospitals, in the inner cities and overseas mission, but all of them are dedicated to strengthening their own prayer lives and those of others. Most of the religious orders schedule regular retreat weekends that are open to all, and most orders also are glad to welcome individuals for a few days or longer to spend quiet time following their own plan or with the guidance of a member of the order. Most of the orders also have a "third order" for men and women who wish to be associated with the order and follow a rule of life designed for people living "in the world." Some retreat centers are sponsored by religious orders, others are owned by dioceses, and some are operated by independent groups within the church, but most offer regular retreats for any who wish to come, and many are able to welcome guests for retreats either on a self-guided or directed basis.

A wide variety of other resources can also be found by those looking for support in their spiritual life. Cursillo weekends, a program that began in the Roman Catholic Church in Spain, have played a very special role in some dioceses and parishes,

as has the Marriage Encounter program. The healing ministry
is also an important part of the life of many Episcopal churches,
sometimes as a regular part of a weekday service and occasionally on Sundays as well. Anointing and praying for the
sick was a central part of Jesus' ministry and continued to be
part of the life of the early church (see Acts 5:15–16 and
James 5:14). Episcopal churches also host weekly meetings of
Alcoholics Anonymous, provide space for pastoral counseling
centers, and offer various "Twelve Step" programs and support groups.

An old rhyme says:

Men's faces, voices, differ much;
Saints are not all one size;
Flow'rs in a garden various grow;
Let none monopolize.

"Saints are not all one size," but each "flower," each member of the body, has its own potential that needs to be nour-
ished. The Episcopal Church has a unique ability to recognize
the diversity of gifts God gives us and, through the rich variety of resources drawn from the experience of the church in
every age and place, to make available the nourishment that
each one needs.

---

1. Att. Patrick (372-466), "St. Patrick's Breastplate," *The Hymnal
1982* (New York: The Church Hymnal Corporation, 1985), 370.

2. Cecil Frances Alexander, "All Things Bright and Beautiful," *The
Hymnal 1982* (New York: The Church Hymnal Corporation, 1985), 405.

QUESTIONS FOR FURTHER
THOUGHT AND DISCUSSION:

1. If you could place some of the sources from which the
Episcopal Church drew on a spectrum from more intuitive to
more rigorous ("right-brained" to "left-brained") it might look
roughly like this:

MYSTIC   CELTIC   ORTHODOX   BENEDICTINE   ROMAN

How do you see your own faith life being influenced by these
backgrounds? What parts of the spectrum draw you, and
which do not? Why?

2. Do you agree with this statement on page 85: "The evangelical insistence on the reality of the sin that alienates human
beings from their Creator, making them dependent on God's
redeeming grace, provides essential balance to a creation-
Incarnation focus that can begin to substitute reason for faith"?
Would you place yourself more on the sin/redemption side or
more on the creation/Incarnation side of this question?

3. What are the three strands of prayer for church members
as explained in this chapter, and how do the first two come to
bear on the third? Which of the three is most important to you
personally? Why?

4. How do you use the Book of Common Prayer? Do you
engage in, or have you ever considered, praying the Daily
Office? Why or why not?

The Church's
Ministry and Organization

MINISTRY

If you look up the word "episcopal" in a dictionary, you will find something like this: "any of various churches governed by bishops, as the Episcopal Church or Anglican Churches." That definition, however, is wrong. The Episcopal Church in the United States of America is not a church governed by bishops; it is in fact governed by a combination of bishops, priests, and lay people elected by the membership of the church to take that responsibility. The Methodist Church is more nearly an episcopal church in the dictionary sense since its bishops have authority to assign clergy to a particular church. The Roman Catholic Church also is an episcopal church in some ways; its bishops have greater authority within their dioceses than do those of the Episcopal Church. But Roman Catholic bishops are subject to the bishop of Rome, so the government of the Roman Catholic Church is really "papal" rather than "episcopal."

The dictionary describes an episcopal church as one in which the bishop is primarily one who governs, but the Prayer Book tells us that the ministry of a bishop is "to represent Christ and his Church… to guard the faith… to proclaim the

Word of God… to act in Christ's name for the reconciliation
of the world and the building up of the Church"(p. 855). It
says nothing about sitting behind a desk and issuing orders. Of
course, at the beginning of the third millennium, it is hard to
imagine a bishop who has no office and never meets with a
committee. Nevertheless, administration is not necessarily the
bishop's primary function.

In the very first days of the church's life, the apostles recognized the conflict between the work of ministry and the need
of organization. "It is not right," they said, "for us to leave
preaching the word of God in order to keep accounts" (Acts
6:2),[1] and bishops in every age have felt that same conflict. In
the long history of the church, therefore, various models of
episcopal ministry have been developed. The Celtic Church
made abbots the administrators and confined bishops to a
sacramental function. The Episcopal Church, early in its history, selected men to go west as bishops who would serve first
of all as missionaries. Some contemporary bishops in the
Episcopal Church see themselves primarily as pastors and del-
egate much of the administrative work to others; others see
themselves first as teachers or evangelists. Bishops, quite naturally, have a variety of gifts, and no two will exercise their ministry in exactly the same way, but few would see their chief
responsibility as "governing." Members of the Episcopal
Church, if asked, would probably say they value bishops most
for two roles: their symbolic role in uniting the church historically with the apostles, and their pastoral leadership in the
diocese. Bishops are, first of all, ministers. They have a ministry to perform, a way of serving God in the church.

If we begin by thinking of bishops as ministers, we will
quickly see that they have a close relationship with all the
church's members, since all members of the Episcopal Church
are called to be ministers. The Prayer Book tells us that "the

ministers of the church are lay persons, bishops, priests, and deacons." The church is a community of people gathered to worship and serve. To define church in terms of government is to miss the point entirely. The primary role of all members—bishops, priests, deacons, and lay people—is ministry: serving God both in the church and in the world.

In St. Paul's letters to the first Christian communities, he has much to say about ministry and the various forms it takes. Although he uses the term "apostle" as a title given to certain specific individuals, he also speaks of the various gifts God gives to people who have ministries without titles: ministries of healing, teaching, leading, assisting, exhorting, giving. Paul shows us a church in which all the members are given gifts for a wide variety of ministries. Within a generation or two, that vision had changed, and the letters of church leaders at the beginning of the second century speak of the three ordained ministries of bishops, priests, and deacons. Later, some "minor orders" also developed, but the threefold ministry remained as an agreed pattern until the time of the Reformation. The practice of setting apart some individuals for these roles, however, led Christians to think of "ministry" as the work of the clergy alone. The Reformation set out to change that and break down the division between clergy and lay people, yet once again the same way of thinking asserted itself. Today, even the churches that once argued for the elimination of distinctions between clergy and lay people have come to use the term "minister" to refer to the individuals who preach and conduct services. Only in recent years has the idea of ministry as the work of all Christians begun to be rediscovered. "Lay ministry" is now much talked about and some small beginnings have been made in learning what it means. A number of dioceses and seminaries now have programs designed to discern, develop, and support lay ministries.

Lay ministry is not about simply assisting clergy. There are, of course, many lay ministries involved in the church's worship and organizational life. Acolytes, lay readers, vestry and Altar Guild members, church school teachers, and so on are all performing valuable ministries, but if the church is to serve the world, it will have to develop a broad range of ministries beyond the church building. Finally, of course, ministry involves the whole life of every Christian. It includes the work Christians do in offices and factories and schools, the way they interact with other people, and the witness they make both publicly and privately by being who they are: members of the body of Christ and God's servants in the world.

When the Book of Common Prayer tells us that the ministers of the church are "lay persons, bishops, priests, and deacons" (p. 855), it makes it clear that lay ministry comes first, and that the other orders are there to support lay members in their work. Although it has been traditional to speak of three orders of "ordained ministry," it is now sometimes suggested that baptism is in reality the ordination of lay people for their ministry. The ministry of the bishop, in succession to the apostles, is described as that of "chief priest and pastor." When Christians gather for worship and a bishop is present, it is the bishop who presides, and it is the bishop who ordains others to carry on the ministry in the local communities. Priests are those who serve primarily in parishes, presiding at the Eucharist, baptizing, teaching, preaching, and supporting the lay people on a daily basis. The ministry of deacons, like that of lay people, has been badly neglected through much of the church's history and has been renewed only in recent years. The deacon has a designated role in the liturgy but a more important role as "servant of those in need" (Prayer Book, p. 856), providing a model of "servant ministry" for all Christians, bringing the compassion of Christ into the lives of those in need.

The church as an organization exists to support and encourage all Christians in their ministries. Since human beings are social animals, some forms of organization are necessary to order our relationships with each other. Organizations are not simply a necessary evil; they enable us to be human, to achieve our full potential. Unfortunately, it is all too easy in the church, as in every human structure, for people to become so involved in maintaining the structure and carrying out the various ministries within it that the world is not served and the primary work of ministry is not done. It is important to know how the work of the church is governed and organized, but it is important also to remember that keeping the vehicle oiled and polished is a pointless activity if it never actually goes anywhere.

THE PARISH CHURCH

How, then, *is* the Episcopal Church governed? The best way to answer that question is to begin with the parish church and with a description of membership. Here we discover a radical difference between the church and secular organizations, which ordinarily define membership in terms of signed applications, approval by the membership, and the payment of dues. Church membership, on the other hand, is defined by baptism: no application, no screening process, and no dues. Membership is normally given to infants who have no idea what is happening and whose qualifications are as yet completely unknown. It is true, unfortunately, that some who are baptized drift away and live for many years without ever attending a service, but if they do come back, they are welcomed home with no questions asked. Like membership in any human family, church membership is organic: it can be dishonored but it cannot be denied.

"The Church," the Prayer Book tells us, "is the Body of which Jesus Christ is the Head and of which all baptized persons

are members" (p. 854). The Episcopal Church takes this definition very seriously: membership is a gift of God and the
church's role is to welcome and nurture, not to create barriers.
Nevertheless, as a practical matter, it is necessary to have membership lists and to define what is meant by "membership."
For this purpose the church has created Canon Law to define
these and other matters. A member of the Episcopal Church,
by this standard, is anyone who has been baptized into the
Episcopal Church or whose baptism in another church has
subsequently been recorded in the Episcopal Church. That
would include a large number of people who have not been to
church in a long time, so there are categories of membership
that include baptized members, communicant members, and
communicant members in good standing. Communicant
members are those who have received communion at least
three times in the previous year. They are in good standing if
they have attended church services regularly and have been
"faithful in working, praying, and giving for the spread of the
Kingdom of God" (Canon I.17.2).

How do these members actually govern the church? The
canons of the Episcopal Church leave that to the individual
states and dioceses. Typically, however, there is an "annual
parish meeting" in which the members of each congregation
come together to elect a vestry to take responsibility for the
finances and property for the coming year. The senior officers
of the vestry, called wardens, may be elected by the parish or
by the vestry itself.

The annual parish meeting also normally provides opportunity for the members of a congregation to be given a full
account of the condition of the parish. The rector may give an
overall picture of the spiritual life of the parish. The wardens
report on the state of the parish from their perspective, the
treasurer of the vestry usually presents a very full financial

report, and leaders of parish organizations report on their activities. Opportunity is usually given also for questions and discussion. In all of this, an Episcopal parish functions as a congregational church, conducting its own affairs as seems appropriate to the members, albeit within the overall diocesan framework.

The canons are clear in dividing the responsibility for parish life between the rector and the vestry. The rector is responsible for the conduct of services and for teaching the faith to children and adults, and the vestry is assigned the management of the finances and the property. Nothing is said in the canons about parish program and outreach ministry. Most vestries, nevertheless, appoint committees to supervise the various aspects of parish life and work with the rector to carry out the parish program. Often the vestry also will establish a worship committee to work with the rector in planning the services so that the priest and people can cooperate in developing a program appropriate to the needs of the community.

One of the most important decisions most parishes need to make is the choice of clergy leadership, and although the parish does choose its rector, it must have the bishop's advice in the process, as well as the bishop's approval of the person selected. When a rector is called to another parish or retires or dies, the parish forms a search committee to look for a new rector. Meanwhile, the vestry, with the advice of the bishop, will select a priest to serve during the period between rectors. In consultation with the diocese, the search committee makes a study of the parish and asks parishioners for their ideas about the needs and opportunities facing the parish. Names of possible candidates are received from the diocese and from the national church, which maintains a computerized list of the clergy with their qualifications and special interests. The search committee reads resumés, visits other parishes, conducts interviews, and finally makes a recommendation to the vestry. When the vestry has elected a priest and received the bishop's approval, the priest is then formally instituted and cannot be removed without due cause and the bishop's consent. It is important for the rector to have that security since it may be necessary for the priest to take controversial positions, and the work of ministry cannot be well done with an eye to popularity. If the parish is financially self-supporting, the priest is called the rector (from a Latin word for "ruler") since he or she usually will preside at meetings of the vestry. New congregations and parishes that are not able to meet all their expenses (sometimes called "mission congregations") will usually have a priest called the vicar (one who *represents* another, in this case the bishop) or priest in charge. The bishop may appoint the priest, though often the appointment is made in consultation with the parish.

The parishes of the Episcopal Church have a considerable degree of independence in managing their affairs and often, especially in cities where there are several Episcopal churches, they will develop a special character in terms of ceremonial and music and outreach ministries. The Episcopal Church assumes that the members of a parish know best what the needs of their community may be and how best to serve that community.

THE DIOCESE

An Episcopal parish is not, however, a congregational church; it is part of a diocese that may include all or part of a state. Dioceses range in size from twenty or thirty parishes up to almost two hundred and provide resources and guidance for the local churches as well as ways for them to work together in common mission. Each parish is assessed an amount of money annually for the work of the diocese. This assessment pays the salaries of the bishop and diocesan staff and supports the work of the church in such tasks as inner-city ministry and planting churches in areas of new population growth. Part of the parish's assessment is passed on to support the work of the national church and the church's mission both in the United States and overseas. Many parishes, however, contribute much more than money for the mission of the church beyond the local community. Parishioners serve on diocesan committees of every variety and work as well in hands-on outreach programs such as soup kitchens and after-school tutoring and in ministries to migrant laborers, to prison inmates, and other special populations.

The work of the diocese is coordinated by an annual convention that elects clergy and lay people to serve on a Diocesan Council. The annual convention adopts a budget and program for the coming year and the Council administers the budget and program. Each parish sends lay delegates to the annual convention. The number of delegates usually is determined by the size of the parish, and all the priests of the diocese are also delegates. In most actions of convention, a simple majority is sufficient, but in electing individuals to various diocesan positions, and in important issues, a majority of both clergy and laity is necessary. It may be an "episcopal church," but little can be done without the consent of the laity.

Just as the bishop has a role in the parish's choice of a priest, so the parish has a role in the selection of a bishop. When a bishop dies or retires or is called to another ministry, a special convention of the diocese is called to choose a successor. Each parish is entitled to send one or more representatives to vote in the diocesan convention, and all priests qualified under diocesan rules are also voting members of the convention. Usually, a nominating committee is formed to receive resumés and interview potential candidates. Convention delegates also are normally given the opportunity to meet the candidates in advance of the convention itself. In the election of a bishop, it is required that a candidate have a majority of the votes of both the clergy and lay delegates. Large dioceses may elect additional bishops called "suffragans" to assist the diocesan bishop, who also may call on a retired bishop to serve as an assistant. A bishop approaching retirement age will often ask the diocese to elect a successor, called a "coadjutor," to serve with him or her in an interim period so that there can be a smooth transition to new leadership.

THE NATIONAL CHURCH

The diocese, with lay people, bishops, priests, and deacons all serving in their various ministries, has always been the basic building block of the church. Yet a diocese never stands alone; it is always joined with other dioceses in an archdiocese, metropolitan area, or national church, which in turn is still only part of the whole church, the Body of Christ. The Council of Nicaea in A.D. 325 provided that no bishop could be consecrated except by three other bishops, thus ensuring that the ministry within each diocese had the approval and support of the larger church. In the Episcopal Church today, the election of a bishop must have the approval of a majority of the other dioceses, and each bishop is consecrated by at least three other bishops of the Episcopal Church.

As the work of the church in each diocese is directed by a bishop and council elected by the diocesan convention, so the work of the national church is governed by a Presiding Bishop and Executive Council elected at a General Convention of the Episcopal Church, held every three years. Those who created the national structure of the Episcopal Church in 1789 were, in many cases, the same individuals who had framed and adopted the Constitution of the United States only a few years earlier. It is not surprising, therefore, to find that the two structures have striking similarities. Like the Congress of the United

States, the General Convention meets in two houses: a House of Bishops, in which all bishops, including assistants, retired bishops, and those in non-diocesan ministries, have voice and vote; and a House of Deputies in which each diocese is represented by four lay deputies and four clerical deputies chosen by their diocesan conventions. The General Convention adopts a budget for the national church, chooses the majority of the members of an Executive Council to administer the budget and to act for the church between conventions, adopts resolutions on matters of concern to church members, and takes action on other matters ranging from the adoption of Prayer Book and Hymnal revisions to ecumenical relationships.

Until the twentieth century, the Presiding Bishop of the Episcopal Church was simply the senior member of the House of Bishops. In simpler times, when the Presiding Bishop's principal duty was to preside at sessions of the General Convention once every three years, he continued to act as bishop of a diocese. Today the role of Presiding Bishop is far more demanding, and the bishop chosen for the position resigns from his or her diocese to serve full-time in that role. The Presiding Bishop serves as chief pastor and chief executive of the church and is charged by the canons with responsibility to "speak God's words to the Church and to the world, as the representative of this Church and its episcopate in its corporate capacity" (Canon I.2 .4[a]). He or she also is called on to visit every diocese and consult with the bishops and diocesan representatives.

The dioceses of the church are grouped in nine provinces in the belief that groups of dioceses can work together in common mission in their regions. Provinces have no specifically assigned roles; therefore, their activities vary greatly. Some, however, have been very effective in coordinating such ministries as those to college students and ethnic groups in their areas of the country.

The Episcopal Church consists not only of the dioceses in the fifty states, but also of a certain number of overseas dioceses that are the result of its missionary work and that, presumably, will become independent churches at some point. At one time, there were dioceses in the Philippines, Africa, Japan, and China that were part of the American Episcopal Church, but these have now been established as part of the national churches in those areas. In recent years two new provinces have been established—one for the dioceses of the Episcopal Church in Mexico and a second for a group of dioceses located in Haiti, the Dominican Republic, Honduras, Colombia, and Ecuador. The latter involves five countries in which English is not the primary language. All this raises an old question with new urgency: why should such a church be called "Anglican"? It is an identity problem that the worldwide Anglican Communion (see below) must face, as its membership becomes predominantly not only non-English but also non-Caucasian.

Beyond the geographical dioceses of the church is an area of four western states within four other dioceses designated as Navajoland, with a bishop chosen to minister to the Navajo people, as well as a Convocation of parishes in Europe that primarily serve Americans living in major cities. The Bishop for the Armed Forces is responsible for supervising the work of Episcopal military chaplains and chaplains in veterans' hospitals and federal prisons.

THE ANGLICAN COMMUNION

Having worked our way from the parish level to the national church, there is still one more level to consider. The Episcopal Church is a member of what is called the worldwide Anglican Communion: a family of churches spread around the world and sharing a common understanding of the Christian faith.

This Communion came into existence in two stages and may now be approaching a third stage of life. In the first stage, explorers and colonists went out from England to settle land in North America, Australia, New Zealand, and elsewhere. Taking their church with them, these colonists quite naturally established branches of the Church of England wherever they went. In time, as in the United States, many of these colonial churches took responsibility for their own government and became sister churches of the Church of England.

The second stage of development, in the nineteenth and twentieth centuries, came as missionaries from England, the United States, and other former colonies were sent out to areas such as China and Japan that had never been part of the British Commonwealth or of the European or American colonial system. In time, new churches developed in these areas as well and became full-fledged members of the family.

Thus an Anglican family of churches came into existence though no one could honestly claim that it had been either planned or expected. Anglicans took their faith with them and knew they had an obligation to share it with others, gradually becoming a family of independent churches bound together by a common heritage and a common understanding of the faith. By the middle of the nineteenth century, people began to recognize that this family existed. The Church in Canada suggested that it would be useful for the bishops of these churches to come together for occasional consultation so that they could maintain their unity and work together toward common goals. As a result, the Archbishop of Canterbury, as the senior member of the family, issued an invitation for the bishops to meet with him at his residence in London, Lambeth Palace. The first such conference, known as the Lambeth Conference, took place in 1867 and was attended by eighty-seven bishops. Since that time, Lambeth Conferences have been held every ten years except in time of war. Some eight hundred bishops attended the Conference in 1998. For the first time, some of the bishops were women; also for the first time, bishops from Africa and Asia outnumbered those from Europe and North America. The Anglican Communion today is a diverse, international body with a membership more geographically diverse than that of any church except the Roman Catholic.

It is at the international level that the nature of the church as an organization becomes most difficult to analyze. The various provinces of the Anglican Communion have their own patterns of self-government, but internationally there has been no structure except the meetings of the Lambeth Conference, and that, as the name implies, is designed for conferring, not legislating. While the bishops may issue statements of their opinions on matters of national, international, or pastoral concern, each national church or province remains free to make its own decisions about its common life. In recent years, however, some additional structures have been put in place. Twice in the last half of the twentieth century, "Anglican Congresses" were held with representation of priests and lay people as well as bishops, but these also were not legislative bodies. More recently, an Anglican Consultative Council, with an elected membership of bishops, priests, and lay people, has been organized to provide regular consultation between the members of the Communion, and an Anglican Executive Officer has been chosen to improve communications between the member churches. But the Anglican Communion remains an international church without a governing body. Some would argue that this is an impractical and unworkable arrangement and that sooner or later a governing body will become necessary. Others maintain that the world of the third millennium, with instant communication between individuals in a "global village," will make an authoritative superstructure a greater impediment to the church's work than an asset. The Roman Catholic Church is finding it increasingly difficult to maintain order; perhaps a church that is more of an organism than an organization will be better able to respond rapidly and effectively to the needs of the future world. "You are the body of Christ," St. Paul wrote to the Christians in Corinth, "and individually members of it" (1 Corinthians 12:27). That same description has always been set out in the Prayer Book Catechism. It is an understanding of the church as a living body, not a bureaucracy; such a way of functioning will frustrate those who prefer the clear lines of authority of an organizational chart. But God made organisms, not organizations, and experience tells us that it is wiser in the long run to accept God's pattern than to create our own.

QUESTIONS FOR FURTHER
THOUGHT AND DISCUSSION:

1. As stated on page 99, the early church is shown by Paul to
be one "in which all the members are given gifts for a wide
variety of ministries. Within a generation or two, that vision
had changed, and the letters of church leaders at the beginning
of the second century speak of the three ordained ministries of
bishops, priests, and deacons." What do you suppose happened to cause the creation of these ordained ministries? What
signs, if any, do you see that might show a return to a stronger
lay ministry in your church?

2. This chapter stresses the Episcopal belief that ministry is
not the work of the clergy alone, but of all members of the
church. Do you agree with the notion that all members are
equipped, or gifted, for special tasks? What are ways in which
people discover their gifts? What particular areas of ministry
do you think you are gifted to perform?

3. In what specific ways is your church connected to the
national level of the Episcopal Church and to the Anglican
Communion? Do you agree with the view presented on page
111 that "the world of the third millennium, with instant
communication between individuals in a 'global village,' will
make an authoritative superstructure a greater impediment to
the church's work than an asset"? Why or why not?

---

1. The Greek text can be translated either "keep accounts" or "wait
on tables."

The Church's Mission

When the first English Prayer Book was issued in 1549, it was described in the preface as a means of unity: from now on, it said, "all the whole realm shall have but one use." The peasants of Cornwall, however, picked up their pitchforks and marched on London rather than accept this new book. From their perspective, since they spoke Cornish and understood English no better than Latin, the imposition of an English-language book was an act of imperialism, an attempt on the part of the English to destroy the Cornish culture. What seemed like a means of unity to authorities in London was unwelcome uniformity to the Cornish. Unity is not the same thing as uniformity, nor can it be imposed from above.

What is it, then, that creates unity? Surely it is not a style of architecture or the arrangement of the furniture. In matters like these, it may be important to use what is familiar to the people the church hopes to serve. Yet different people may see this matter very differently. A Canadian missionary in Japan in the mid-twentieth century, for example, built a church in a village where no church had been before. He had it built in the Japanese style with rice straw mats (*tatami*) on the floor for people to sit on, a low table for an altar, and pottery vessels for Communion. He hoped to introduce the people to Christianity in a setting that was familiar to them rather than in a thick covering of western culture. When he left, however, a Japanese priest was assigned to the church, and the new priest took up the tatami mats and put down a wooden floor. He installed a high altar, bought metal vessels for Communion, provided wooden pews for people to sit on, and made the church look like those he had visited in England. It seemed to him that the Canadian priest had not introduced full-fledged Christianity since he had not done things the way the English do. Whether either priest consulted the people of the village or which approach gained more response is not clear.

Christians at the beginning of the third millennium are more sensitive to the differences between ethnic groups than previous generations. As the world is transformed, though, into a global village in which blue jeans, sneakers, and T-shirts are the international costume and the same television programs are watched in the high plains of Tibet and the Amazon jungle, it will be increasingly difficult for the Christian Church to distinguish between those elements that are essential for unity and those that reflect unexamined western traditions and assumptions. Christians concerned with preserving ethnic traditions may find themselves trying to hold on to traditions that those who developed them are quite ready to abandon. We cannot assume, either, that there is still a standard or "norm" in the Episcopal Church or Anglican Communion at the beginning of the third millennium. There are American congregations in which the singing is supported by guitars and the other instruments of popular culture, and there are other congregations content to sing Victorian hymns accompanied by the traditional organ. The first English Prayer Book was published to enable people to pray in their own language, but the Cornish were overlooked. In the Episcopal Church today there are Prayer Books in many languages, hymnals of various styles, and a wide range of ceremonial manners, all intended to communicate one gospel—though the differences make some church members wonder whether there can be unity with so much diversity.

"The mission of the Church," says the Prayer Book, "is to restore all people to unity with God and each other in Christ" (p. 855). But how is that unity to be expressed and attained? In the emerging global village of the twenty-first century, sensitivity to human diversity is greater than ever before but perhaps more difficult to cope with because the distances between cultures are so much smaller. Prayer Books and bishops once seemed enough to unite us, but in the newly revised Prayer Books of the Anglican Communion, there is increasing divergence from the original model, and when the bishops of the Communion assemble every ten years, there is a growing diversity of language, culture, theological orientation, and mission priorities. Whatever uniformity there may once have been has almost disappeared and the unity is harder than ever to discern. Nonetheless, the church is committed to unity and its efforts toward that goal may be seen in three primary areas: world mission, social mission, and the ecumenical movement.

UNITY THROUGH MISSION

Jesus gave his disciples two clear commands. The first command, "Do this in remembrance of me" (Luke 22:19), is fulfilled in the eucharistic gathering; the second, "Go therefore and make disciples of all nations, baptizing them in the name of the Father and of the Son and of the Holy Spirit, and teaching them to obey everything that I have commanded you" (Matthew 28:19–20), was understood by the first Christians as a command to go throughout the world with the good news of God's forgiveness and the gift of new life in Christ. In the face of Roman persecution (but with the assistance of Roman roads and order), they carried the gospel to places as far from Jerusalem as England and Ethiopia and India in those early years. By the beginning of the fourth century Christianity had become the strongest movement in the Roman Empire. Persecution had been intended to unify the empire by eliminating dissident groups like the Christians, but when Constantine ended the persecution of the church in A.D. 315 it was at least in part because he realized that Christianity might do more to unify the empire if it were allowed instead to flourish.

But Constantine was in for a surprise. Under conditions of persecution, Christians had developed different understandings of the faith in different parts of the empire, and the end of persecution brought these differences into the open. It was in order to unite the church that Constantine called the Council of Nicaea, and the Council responded by adopting an official creed: Christians would for the first time find their unity in a statement of belief.

With Constantine's support, the church grew rapidly in the Roman Empire, but the work of mission beyond the empire proceeded slowly. The western church in particular had all it could do to cope with the barbarians flooding down from the north. Pope Gregory sent Augustine to England at the end of the sixth century, Cyril and Methodius carried the gospel to the Slavs of eastern Europe in the ninth century, and the conversion of Russia began in the tenth century, but there were still pagan areas of Europe at the end of the Middle Ages. The great age of European exploration that began in the fourteenth century opened Asia to the Christian church, and Francis Xavier reached Japan in 1549. Nevertheless, at every stage of the Christian mission there was controversy about the nature of unity. Although Gregory instructed Augustine to preserve what was good in the customs of the pagan Angles, the Christian customs of the Celts were finally set aside in favor of those of Rome, Methodius was put in prison for translating the liturgy into Slavonic, and historians still debate what might have happened if the Jesuit missionaries in China in the sixteenth century had been allowed to connect the veneration of ancestors with the veneration of Christian saints. It was hard for Christians to identify and interpret what was essential to their faith in terms of the customs of the countries and cultures in which they served.

The work of mission was both encouraged and impeded by the creation of colonial empires in the eighteenth and nineteenth centuries. It was not always clear whether European governments were supporting Christianity or Christianity was enabling the rule of European governments. English missionaries sometimes preceded but more often followed the flag, planting churches in India, Africa, Australia, and, with missionaries from the United States and Canada, in China and Japan. Until the Hymnal was revised in 1982, Episcopalians sang triumphant hymns that told them how, "From Greenland's icy mountains / From India's coral strand /... From many an ancient river / From many a palmy plain / They call us to deliver / Their land from error's chain."[1] But for all the narrowness of the view such hymns expressed, the missionaries were passionate about the gospel and deeply committed to serving the people to whom they went. They not only built churches uniting more people in a common faith, but also established schools and hospitals bringing standards of education and health care that previously had been unknown in many areas.

The Episcopal Church in the nineteenth century had most of a continent as a mission field. Well into the second half of the twentieth century a number of western states were still officially described as "missionary districts." Mexico, Central America, much of the Caribbean area, and even Brazil and the Philippines were also spheres of mission for the Episcopal Church. Missionaries home on "furlough" traveled about informing church members of their work and encouraging support. At least a third of the budget of the Episcopal Church for many years was devoted to missionary work at home and abroad.

The last third of the twentieth century, however, saw the beginning of a radical reorientation. The new churches planted by Anglican missionaries in Africa, Asia, and Latin America were becoming independent members of the Anglican Communion with their own leadership. Fundamental questions were beginning to arise about the very nature of the missionary enterprise. Although there were still unevangelized areas in the Amazon region and New Guinea, most of the younger churches could now train their own leadership, and Americans, who sometimes did not speak the language and appeared on the scene as well-intentioned outsiders, could no longer make a very significant difference. If, as someone once said, "the church exists by mission as a fire exists by burning," how could the church exist without mission? The Anglican Congress of 1963 in Toronto brought together clergy and lay people from the various churches of the communion to discuss the problem and issued a call for "Mutual Responsibility and Interdependence in the Body of Christ." Mission would continue, but as a two-way street, through the sharing of resources and vision between the older and younger churches.

It was also true that the new churches created by the missionaries often had a rather different understanding of the faith than those who had converted them. By the time of the Lambeth Conference of 1998 these differences had erupted into significant tensions and potential divisions. African church leaders, trained as missionaries by missionaries, were still focused on mission. Their churches were growing rapidly while Anglican churches in England, Canada, and the United States had turned inward, concerned with such issues as the ordination of women, the acceptance of homosexuals, and the problem of ethnic divisions within their societies. Some of the most important missionary work of the church in American communities was now being done among new-comers from Latin America and Asia, and American dioceses were surprised to find that they now had work going on at home in many languages.

A further problem created by the new situation of the churches was the relationship between Christianity and the other great world religions that not only had not disappeared (as some expected they would) but seemed to have gained new energy. How should the mission "to bring all people into unity in Christ" be understood in a time of resurgent Islam? Islam, the bishops at Lambeth learned, can be very different in different parts of the world. British and American bishops who were beginning to work on neighborly relations with the leaders of the new mosques in their communities heard reports of persecution of Christians by Moslems in the Sudan and elsewhere. Does "unity" require making conversion of non-Christians always the first priority, or is it possible that through dialogue among the world's religions problems of ethnic tension can be more easily resolved? Might a deeper understanding of apparent differences lead to a unity like that envisioned by St. Paul, in which various branches are grafted at last into a common root (Romans 11:17–24)?

We live in a time of transition from one missionary era to another. Where once the Episcopal Church supported hundreds of missionaries in other countries, today a small handful still serve under that title. A program called Volunteers for

Mission sends Episcopalians with particular skills in response
to requests from other Anglican churches, and a companion
diocese program links many American dioceses to dioceses of
sister churches. Under the heading of Partners in Mission, the
churches of the Anglican Communion are beginning to
explore ways to work together, learning from each other, sharing resources, and exchanging personnel. The work of mission
is not dead but different. The great accomplishments of the
past provide very little guidance for the work we are called
to now. The complexity of the missionary challenge of the
twenty-first century will demand more wisdom and commitment from Christians than ever before.

UNITY IN SOCIETY

When the Jewish people looked at the world around them,
they saw that it was rigidly divided by race, language, culture,
and class. It seemed to them that this arrangement was unnat-
ural. If, as they believed, there was one Creator who created
one original couple, why should there be such divisions within the human race? "Have we not all one father?" asked the
prophet Malachi, "has not one God created us?" To explain
our situation, they told the story of the Tower of Babel, which
asserts that human divisions are the result of human pride
(Genesis 11:1–9). Thousands of years later, no one has suggested a better answer. More important than the explanation of
our divisions, however, is the remedy. The Old Testament clearly indicates God's will for a final human unity (see Isaiah 49:6b,
Isaiah 60:3, and Malachi 1:11), and Christians trace the origins
of their church to an event that vividly portrayed God's intention to accomplish that purpose. On the day of Pentecost, the
apostles were driven out into the streets of Jerusalem to proclaim the gospel, and all who heard them, whatever their nation
or language, could understand the message (Acts 2). Before

long, they began to see also that there could be no more divisions between Jews and Gentiles in the church, or between male and female, or between those who were slaves and those who were free (Galatians 3:28).

It was a hard lesson to learn and the Epistle of James rebukes those who have failed to understand (2:1–7), but it was clear to the early Christians that the gospel of Jesus had to do with a God who blessed the poor (Luke 6:20) and put down the mighty and sent the rich away empty (Luke 1:52–53). That gospel appealed especially to the slaves and outcasts of the Roman Empire (1 Corinthians 1:26–28), and although the church would become rich and powerful itself, the gospel continued to draw people like Francis of Assisi, who renounced his wealth to preach to the outcasts of his day, and Mother Teresa of Calcutta, who cared for the poorest of the poor in twentieth century Calcutta.

The Reformation of the Church of England took place in part because Henry VIII wanted to acquire the wealth of the church and in part because leaders like Bishop Hugh Latimer were offended by it. As an established church, the Church of England continued to have access to wealth and power but also to feel a responsibility to the whole of society. Again and again, the church has produced reformers to demand that working conditions be improved, that the needy be cared for, that schools be created to educate children and hospitals to care for those who are sick. Those who look at society through the eyes of Christ have continued to see new ways to serve. William Wilberforce worked to abolish the slave trade, Florence Nightingale created the modern profession of nursing, and, in the last half of the twentieth century, the modern hospice movement began with the work of Dame Cicely Saunders, who founded St. Christopher's Hospice in London.

The Episcopal Church, closely connected as it has been to the Church of England, has displayed the same tendencies toward wealth and power on the one hand and a concern for the needs of society as a whole on the other. Though it is often incorrectly assumed that the Episcopal church is the wealthiest in the country, there are certainly many wealthy Episcopal churches. Trinity Church, Wall Street, not only owns and profits from some of the most valuable real estate in the world, but it also has a grant-making program that provides assistance to churches not only in the United States but in Africa and many other parts of the world.

The most effective agency of the whole church for response to human need is undoubtedly the Presiding Bishop's Fund for World Relief. Created both to respond to immediate needs and to work toward the long-term solution of problems of disease and natural disaster, the Fund's agenda to help seems to come from the Great Litany in the Prayer Book: "earthquake, fire, and flood... plague, pestilence, and famine... oppression... violence" (p. 149). The Fund allocates more than a million dollars in a typical year for emergency assistance, for instance, to victims of hurricanes in Honduras and tornadoes in Texas, while being involved in long-term projects as diverse as vocational training in Ethiopia, health care for Mexican children, and solar energy development. Personal involvement is high on the agenda and the Fund tries to link churches and individuals with specific projects. Church members can support a specific project or go themselves to help build housing or provide other skills in devastated areas.

Our review of the church's history has already noted the impact of the social gospel on the church in the nineteenth century and the fact that Episcopal churches in the urban areas led in the establishment of hospitals and social centers serving the needs of the poor. Of the twelve colleges affiliated with the Episcopal Church, three are "historically black" colleges in

Virginia, North Carolina, and South Carolina, founded after the Civil War to provide access to higher education for those recently freed from slavery, and one is an institution in Chicago founded in the 1980s to provide opportunities for Hispanic people of the inner city. William Muhlenberg's pioneering institution, St. Luke's Hospital, New York, was the first hospital to follow Dame Cicely Saunders's lead and create a hospice program in this country.

Today there are hundreds of health and welfare agencies affiliated with the Episcopal Church: numerous hospitals, some serving special groups such as children or recovering alcoholics, counseling centers and schools for troubled teenagers, shelters for victims of domestic abuse and for runaway young people, homes for orphaned children, and retirement homes for the elderly. There are agencies to make loans to improve housing in rural areas and the inner city, and agencies to teach such skills as agriculture and automotive mechanics to young people to help them become self-sufficient. Many parishes in communities of every size also operate food pantries and soup kitchens. The largest soup kitchen in the country, at Holy Apostles' Church, New York City, provides thousands of meals every week and helps people find the guidance they need to begin putting their lives back together. To coordinate and encourage programs of this sort, the Episcopal Church has given recognition to "Jubilee Centers" throughout the country where effective programs of social ministry are being carried out. In the closing years of the twentieth century, the Episcopal Church has also provided leadership in ministry to those affected by AIDS and helped people understand the dimensions of the problem through services of witness and intercession.

Inevitably, a social conscience creates controversy. If the Epistle of James had to scold Christians in the first century of the church's life for catering to the rich and neglecting the poor, it is not surprising to find that the gospel's special concern for the poor and outcast continues to create divisions. In the turmoil of the 1960s, the Presiding Bishop, John Hines, created turmoil in the church when he called on the General Convention of the church to create a special program to make grants to those without power in American society. Power given to some is power taken from others, and those who felt threatened by the program were quick to make their voices heard. Edmond Browning, who served as Presiding Bishop from 1986 to 1997, created controversy by reaching out to people with AIDS and to homosexuals. His goal of a church with "no outcasts" made some members of the church feel like outcasts themselves. There are always some who look to the church as a place of peace and refuge from the troubles of the world; yet, oddly, it is the church's effort to provide refuge to those who seem to need it most that tends to cause the most difficulty.

Further division is caused when church members become involved in the political process. "Separation of church and state" is a basic precept of American life, but there are widely varying visions of what that means. Many church members feel that the church's concern for justice must inevitably include a concern for changing unjust laws. Why, they ask, should the church continue to feed the hungry but make no effort to create and support government programs that might enable people to find good jobs and buy food for themselves? Others would argue that Jesus fed the hungry and healed the sick but declined to lead a rebellion against the government. Episcopalians, again perhaps because of their English establishment heritage, have generally felt more comfortable than members of many other churches in calling attention to laws that ought to be changed and working to change them. The church maintains a Washington office to call attention to issues of concern to church members and to facilitate communication between members of the church and members of Congress. This, too, is controversial.

It is ironic that the church's efforts "to restore all people to unity with God and each other in Christ" should cause so much division, but Jesus' ministry also was controversial and for the same reasons. He associated often with the poor and the outcast, and the more respectable members of society complained about it to his disciples. Jesus' response was, "Those who are well have no need of a physician, but those who are sick; I have come to call not the righteous but sinners to repentance" (Luke 5:31–32). Following Jesus' example will often create the same controversy today that it caused then, but there will be more unity in a society that cares for all its members than in a society in which divisions of race and class go unrecognized and unhealed. There will always be controversy about the methods by which this ministry is carried out, but there can be no question of the centrality of this ministry to the gospel.

If the Episcopal Church is to keep faith with the gospel, there inevitably will be differences of opinion about methods and priorities, and these should be vigorously, even angrily, debated. The call to unity is not about uniformity of approach but about unity in obedience to the gospel. There were divisions also in the church in Corinth, and St. Paul suggested that the church is a body with many members who have many different roles to play. No member of the Body of Christ can say to another member, "I have no need of you" (1 Corinthians 12:12–27). Uniformity of opinion and vision might be more comfortable to some, but unity is made up of diversity. It is precisely in the clash of opinions and the debating of different visions that the mission of the church is clarified. A church without controversy would be a dead church. The Episcopal Church at the beginning of the third millennium is far from dead!

UNITY OF CHRISTIANS

At the last meal shared with the disciples before his death, Jesus prayed "that they may all be one... so that the world may believe that you have sent me" (John 17:21). Divisions, however, began almost at once. Among the first converts were Greek-speaking Jews and Aramaic-speaking Jews, and it seemed to those who spoke Greek that the widows in their group were being neglected (Acts 6:1). Later Sts. Peter and Paul argued bitterly over what was to be required of Gentile converts to the Christian faith (Acts 15:4–11). In the fourth century, the Council of Nicaea was called to resolve the issues dividing the newly legalized church, in seventh-century England a Council met at Whitby to settle differences between the Roman and Celtic patterns of church life, and in the eleventh century the bishops of Rome and Constantinople excommunicated each other, creating a division that has not yet been healed. In the sixteenth century, the Reformation brought renewal to the church but brought deep divisions as well.

The English church, separated by the English Channel from the fierce controversies on the continent, hoped to find a way to unite at least the Calvinists and Lutherans. Archbishop Cranmer worked hard to bring their leaders together to work out their differences, but his efforts failed. In the next century, Archbishop Laud held a famous discussion with "Mr. Fisher, a Jesuit," but without result. Even in England, it proved impossible at last to hold together Christians whose visions of the faith were as different as those of Archbishop Laud and Oliver Cromwell.

Yet the vision of unity has remained at the center of the Anglican understanding of the church's mission. As we have seen already in reviewing the church's history, proposals were made in the middle of the nineteenth century to draw Christian churches together on the basis of four essential elements: Bible, creeds, apostolic ministry, and the sacraments of baptism and Holy Communion. In the 1950s, Eugene Carson Blake of the Presbyterian Church and Bishop James Pike of California called on the churches to begin to implement this proposal, and a Consultation on Church Unity was created involving a number of major American churches. Specific plans have been drawn up, but so far none that would satisfy all the member churches.

If specific proposals to reunite churches of different tradi-tions have failed, a new way forward has begun to be explored that would provide for mutual recognition of members and ministries without proceeding as yet to organic unity. The Evangelical Lutheran Church in America and the Episcopal Church, building on a dialogue that began in 1971, agreed to an "Interim Sharing of the Eucharist" in 1982, and it seems highly likely that by the beginning of the twenty-first century a mutual recognition of ministries will take place. Lutheran bishops henceforward would be consecrated by other bishops in apostolic succession and Lutheran pastors would be ordained only by bishops, thus creating a common pattern of ministry in the two churches. Whether this pattern of unity will lead to further steps remains to be seen, but after centuries of division even such small steps forward are encouraging and give hope for the future.

THE ANGLICAN VISION

Uniquely among the churches, the Anglican vision from the very beginning has been not centered so much on organi-zational unity or doctrinal unity as on a community united in worship. At first, Anglicans looked back to the early centuries of the church to find the essentials around which Christians could be united, but increasingly Anglicans have come to understand that the early church was not united and that the unity God wills for the church lies in the future. As the church moves through history, new challenges arise and old answers become inadequate. Jesus did not tell his disciples that he had left them with all the answers, but rather, "When the Spirit of truth comes, he will guide you into all the truth" (John 16:13). So the discovery of truth is a continuing journey guided by the Holy Spirit, and the answers we find are always provisional answers. They may have been satisfactory in the past but that offers no guarantee that they will be equally satisfactory in the future. Jesus himself is the truth, but statements about Jesus will not necessarily be able to capture the whole of that truth in terms that a changing society needs to hear. Likewise the structures of the church that have been vastly different in different periods of the church's history may need to be further changed to meet the needs of a new millennium. Bishops have been pastors in the Celtic church, administrators in the Roman church, democratic leaders in the American church, yet always symbols of unity across time and space. Episcopalians are confident that bishops will be at the center of any further steps toward unity, though their exact function in a reunited church must still be explored.

Above all, Anglicans have never claimed to be *the* church. On its title page, the Book of Common Prayer says that it contains forms for the "Administration of the Sacraments and Other Rites and Ceremonies of the Church... according to the use of The Episcopal Church." We do it this way, in other words, but we are only a part of the whole church and make no claim that this is the only way. In the words of Canon Edward West, "There are other ways of holiness, but this is the only way I understand." It is, Episcopalians believe, a good way. It is a way, as former Archbishop of Canterbury Michael Ramsey once said, that "converts sinners and creates saints." Until God shows us a better way, that is all we can ask.

QUESTIONS FOR FURTHER
THOUGHT AND DISCUSSION:

1. What were the causes and what are the effects of the "radical reorientation" in mission work described on page 118?

2. In light of Jesus' command to go and make disciples of all nations, what is your response to the question posed on page 119: "Does 'unity' require making conversion of non-Christians always the first priority, or is it possible that through dialogue among the world's religions problems of ethnic tension can be more easily resolved?"

3. What is your opinion of the controversial actions of John Hines and Edmond Browning described on page 124? What criteria should church leaders use to determine whether an issue is important enough to risk turmoil and division?

4. As stated on page 126, divisions in the early church "began almost at once." What have been some of the specific issues that have divided the church? Given the church's propensity for division, how likely do you think it is that the Anglican vision of unity will ever be fulfilled?

------

1. "Hymn 254," *The Hymnal 1940* (New York: The Church Hymnal Corporation, 1940).

Suggestions for Further Reading

ANGLICANISM

Griffiss, James E. *The Anglican Vision*. Boston: Cowley Publications, 1997. Similar in approach to the present book, but dealing with Anglicanism in general rather than the American Episcopal Church.

Webber, Christopher L. *Finding Home: Stories of Roman Catholics Entering the Episcopal Church*. Boston: Cowley Publications, 1997. The stories of priests and lay people of Roman Catholic background who have found a home in the Episcopal Church.

Webber, Robert. *Evangelicals on the Canterbury Trail*. Harrisburg, Pennsylvania: Morehouse Publishing, 1989. Stories of people coming into the Episcopal Church from an evangelical background.

CHURCH HISTORY

Holmes, David. *A Brief History of the Episcopal Church*. Harrisburg, Pennsylvania: Trinity Press, 1993.

Prichard, Robert. *A History of the Episcopal Church*. rev. ed., Harrisburg, Pennsylvania: Morehouse Publishing, 1999.

THE BIBLE

Johnston, Michael. *Engaging the Word*. Boston: Cowley Publications, 1998. An introduction to the methods used in interpreting the Bible today.

WORSHIP

The Book of Common Prayer and Administration of the Sacraments and Other Rites and Ceremonies of the Church: Together with The Psalter or Psalms of David: According to the Use of the Episcopal Church. New York: Church Publishing Incorporated, 1979. Referred to as the Prayer Book throughout this volume.

Mitchell, Leonel L. *Praying Shapes Believing: A Theological Commentary on the Book of Common Prayer.* Harrisburg, Pennsylvania: Morehouse Publishing, 1985. A commentary on the theology of each part of the Book of Common Prayer.

Stevenson, K. and B. Spinks, ed. *The Identity of Anglican Worship.* Harrisburg, Pennsylvania: Morehouse Publishing, 1991. A collection of essays on Anglican worship.

Webber, Christopher L. *A User's Guide to the Book of Common Prayer, The Holy Eucharist Rites I and II.* Harrisburg, Pennsylvania: Morehouse Publishing, 1997. A commentary on the Eucharist placed on facing pages with the text itself, enabling the reader to learn while using the Prayer Book.

Webber, Christopher L. *A User's Guide to the Book of Common Prayer, Morning Prayer and Baptism.* Harrisburg, Pennsylvania: Morehouse Publishing, 1997. A commentary on the services of Morning Prayer and Baptism placed on facing pages with the text itself, enabling the reader to learn while using the Prayer Book.

CHURCH TEACHING

Booty, John. *What Makes Us Episcopalians?* Harrisburg, Pennsylvania: Morehouse Publishing, 1982. A brief pamphlet on key Anglican theological concepts.

McPherson, C. W. *Understanding Faith: An Exploration of Christian Theology.* Harrisburg, Pennsylvania: Morehouse Publishing, 1998. A careful analysis of the way Episcopalians think about the major articles of their faith.

SPIRITUALITY

Guenther, Margaret. *The Practice of Prayer.* Boston: Cowley Publications, 1998. A guide to the basic essentials of prayer.

MISSION

Harris, Mark. *The Challenge of Change: The Anglican Communion in the Post-Modern Era.* New York: Church Publishing, 1998. A study of what Anglicans can contribute to the life of the Christian Church in the next millennium.